Arthur Koestler

The Story of a Friendship

ARTHUR KOESTLER

The Story of a Friendship

George Mikes

ANDRE DEUTSCH

First published 1983 by
André Deutsch Limited
105 Great Russell Street London WC1

Typeset by Inforum Limited, Portsmouth
Printed in Great Britain by
The Thetford Press Limited, Thetford, Norfolk

ISBN 233 97612 4

To Marietta who loved them too

CONTENTS

INTRODUCTION

Having finished this little book I realise, with some surprise, that I have done what I set out to do: I have simply
written the story of my friendship with Arthur Koestler.
Not a biography – there are several of those and Arthur
himself wrote four autobiographical works; not an
appreciation of his writings – his literary achievement is
not my subject, his scientific works are beyond my com-
petence and often beyond my understanding and his
parapsychology bored me to tears.

So am I doing justice to Arthur Koestler? Perhaps not
but that is not my aim here. My view of him is on the trivial
plane, not on the tragic one – as he might put it. He felt
more comfortable on the tragic plane. I am quite happy
on the trivial.

The title of my book *How to be an Alien* could not be
translated into Hungarian and various other languages,
so for those versions I called it *England in Slippers*. This
book is *Arthur Koestler in Slippers*. Biographers, critics,
scientists will write a great deal more about him. These
pages may give them – and the author of the definitive
biography – a few crumbs of data and a little spice. And
they may provide an informal close-up portrait for the
many people who admired him, and recall memories for
the few who knew him well enough to love him dearly.

One day when I was dining with the Koestlers a gush-
ing and over-enthusiastic American lady dropped in for
drinks. She told Arthur how pleased, honoured and
overwhelmed she was to be in the presence of the great
man. When she said it for the fifth time, Arthur told her:

1

'My dear young lady, to like a writer and then to meet the writer is like loving goose-liver and then meeting the goose.'

I knew the goose intimately. And still love goose-liver. That's what this book is really about.

THE LAST GAME

On Monday February 28, 1983, I travelled to Geneva. On Sunday evening – the night before my departure – my friend Marietta and I were invited to the Koestlers for dinner. On such occasions, which were frequent, we appeared at 6 o'clock and played two games of scrabble before dinner, with sometimes a third, after it. Scrabble we played in the dining-room; dinner we had in the kitchen. On this particular occasion our visit would have had another purpose too: we were to deliver a smoked ham, the Koestlers' share of the two pigs we had bought together and which had been killed in December 1982.

On Sunday morning I went to play tennis. Returning at about 12.30 I found a message on my telephone answering machine from Cynthia, asking me to ring them back.

'It's about tonight,' the message said.

When I rang, Cynthia told me that 'Arthur's Parkinson's is bad today,' so he would not be able to play scrabble but we should come for dinner all the same. In the past, when Arthur had been feeling not too well, he had always asked us to postpone the visit entirely. He hated being seen when his hands were trembling and, in any case, he got tired very soon. So I ought to have found this 'come for dinner all the same' a little strange, but I did not.

I told Cynthia: 'Oh no. If Arthur is not well we'll postpone it. I'm back from Switzerland in ten days, then we'll come for dinner *and* play scrabble. The ham can wait too.'

'Splendid,' said Cynthia.

On such occasions she invariably added: 'Wait a minute, Arthur wants to have a word with you.' This time she said nothing. Even in this I found nothing

3

extraordinary. I had just been informed that Arthur was in poor shape.

On Friday morning, on March 4, I was getting dressed in my son's flat in Lausanne, when he phoned me from Geneva, where he works.

'I have very sad news for you,' Martin told me. 'Mr and Mrs Koestler have been found dead in their drawing-room.'

I thanked him for the information and put the receiver down. I cannot say I was stunned or even shocked. I always receive horrible news calmly. I never panic – indeed, the more terrible the event the cooler I become. I am a delayed action man. It is only a few hours, sometimes a few days, later – depending on the power of the blow – that the full impact hits me.

My first thoughts were regret that I did not see them that Sunday. Then I clearly recalled Cynthia's word: 'Splendid!' Now it sounded ominous. I was not sure whether I was imagining it, influenced by the powerful force of hindsight, but now it seemed that her voice had sounded melancholy, even a trifle mocking. She knew – I felt now – that we would not have dinner together ever again. Nor should we ever again play scrabble. Not in this world. Perhaps in the other one which I do not believe in but Arthur did, in a fashion.

Perhaps he was right, I thought – as he so often was during his long and bellicose life – and we would still have a chance of continuing our games: a pleasant outlook for eternity. But rereading once again his thoughts on this matter, I see that according to him, while death does not mean total extinction it does not mean a prolonged heavenly existence either. It means 'merging into cosmic consciousness'. The process of dying is 'the flow of a river into the ocean', he explains. 'The river has been freed of the mud that clung to it and regained its transparency. It has become identified with the sea, spread over it, omnipresent in every drop, catching a spark of the sun.'

A little too imaginative for my prosaic mind; but, whatever I may make of it, this does not sound like games of scrabble on the Elysian fields. What a pity.

ATTILA THE POET

In the autumn of 1952 I wrote a long article for the *Times Literary Supplement* on Endre Ady, the great Hungarian poet who was born seventy-five years earlier. Soon afterwards I left for New York. There I received a letter from Alan Pryce-Jones, editor of the *TLS*, telling me that a friend of his, Arthur Koestler, would like to meet the author of that article and would I agree to the lifting of anonymity (a strict rule of the *TLS* in those days). If I did, would I ring Mr Koestler after my return? I wrote back to Alan saying that anonymity was *his* rule, not mine, and as far as I was concerned he could print my name under (or preferably over) all my contributions. I added that of course I would ring Mr Koestler as soon as I got back.

By that time I was a firm Koestler addict, but I had been only slowly converted. I had seen him once, during the war, when he made a speech for Count Károlyi's Free Hungarian Movement, and found him a disappointing speaker. Like so many other writers, he felt safe at his desk but ill at ease facing a live audience. I do not remember his subject, but I do remember that it was not a stirring speech followed by a tempestuous debate, but altogether rather a dull affair. His Hungarian, though accentless, was occasionally halting and was full of strange phrases, obvious translations from English and – much worse – German.

I knew that he had written one or two famous books but I had not read them. I am afraid I had been put off by other Hungarian writers. Before Koestler's emergence, two Hungarian best-sellers had hit the market, one by

5

Hans Habe and the other by Peter de Polnay. Both books were readable and decently written – even deservedly successful – but to my mind they seemed undistinguished and forgettable. So I was in no hurry to make the acquaintance of a third Hungarian best-selling author, Arthur Koestler.

Soon after that meeting where I heard Koestler speak and became as a consequence even less interested in him than before, I visited some Hungarian friends, George and Kato Frank and I saw Koestler's book *Scum of the Earth* lying about. They offered to lend it to me but I declined with thanks. Kato was surprised, so I explained that I had read Habe and read Polnay and these two books had fully satisfied my need for famous Hungarians writing in English.

Kato smiled and said: 'Just take it. This is quite different.'

She is an educated lady of exquisite taste, so I took the book. When, a few days later, I started reading it, I could not put it down. Then I reread some parts of it. I had no doubt that I had been introduced to a major writer of our age, a man of shining integrity and remarkable talent. I rushed to buy (or more likely, when I come to think of it, to borrow from the Times Book Club) *Darkness at Noon*. If I was impressed and shaken by *Scum of the Earth* (Koestler's description of his time in a French concentration camp) I was bowled over by Rubashov's story. I then read all Koestler's essays I could lay hands on, and a year or two later practically queued up to get one of the first copies of the *Yogi and the Commissar* and *Arrival and Departure*. I have never read – not to this day – his first novel, *The Gladiators*, which is about Spartacus, leader of the Roman slave revolt. I fail to understand why I have refused – or just omitted – to read it: looking through my collection of his books, I see that was the first book I received from him, with a warm and friendly dedication. Perhaps, in the early days, I did not want to spoil the effect of *Darkness at Noon*. Although it seemed probable that *The Gladiators* was a distinguished first novel, I had a strong feeling that Spartacus could not possibly reach the

6

ibly want from me, and he came to the subject straight
away: 'Did you know Attila József?' he asked.

'Yes, I did,' I told him.*

Attila József was a great poet, the last genius among
four or five geniuses who wrote in Magyar, that strange
and isolated language, lost to the world at large. The
son of an unskilled labourer and a charwoman, he was
brought up in dire poverty. He did not even remember
his father who disappeared when he was a small boy.
Attila joined the Communists but was disillusioned by the
Party and became a Trotskyite. When Koestler arrived in
Budapest, in 1935, they became friends and argued a
great deal. Koestler was a devout, orthodox Communist
and strongly disapproved of Attila's heresy. These argu-
ments never spoiled their friendship, mostly because they
did not take each other's politics too seriously. Koestler
was a cosmopolitan, who had travelled widely in the
Soviet Union, expected the salvation of the world by the
Creed and was preoccupied by the threat of Nazism.
Attila did not care a damn about the Soviet Union and
although he was watching the rise of the Nazis with deep
anxiety and an even deeper disgust, he was really concerned with the suffering, misery and near starvation of
his own people, the Magyar proletariat. His own short life
was haunted with poverty. Koestler wrote: 'He never
achieved the "monthly two hundred" which became one
of his various obsessions. The "two hundred" refers to
Hungarian pengoes and the total of the unattainable
dream was the equivalent of twelve pounds per month.'

Attila became mad, suffering from schizophrenia, and
killed himself forty-six years before his friend, Koestler.

Trains were another of Attila's obsessions, and trains –
especially goods trains – keep rumbling through his

* I may be reproached by some pedantic people for 'inventing' the
bits of dialogue in this book. To this silly charge I shall not give the
even sillier reply that I have total recall and remember every word.
While I have a pretty good memory for conversations, I most
certainly do not remember the exact words in all cases and I would
not write dialogue if I were writing history. The words quoted,
however, are always very near the actual words used, and it seems to
me that the use of dialogue makes a text more lively and readable.

poetry. In 1937, having spent a few weeks in a mental hospital, he was deemed fit to be released to the care of his sisters who lived by Lake Balaton. He kept going to the railway station to watch trains. One day he saw a goods train leaving the station. He broke into a run, caught up with the slowly moving train and laid his right arm on the rail, between two carriages. But the train demanded more than just an arm: the carriage hit his head and the poet was killed instantaneously. The severed right arm was later found at some distance.

Koestler, always a master of horror, adds to this story: 'A few days after Attila's death, his family found in his drawer a shirt from which the right sleeve had been cut off with scissors. His guilt-complex had apparently inspired him with the idea that he must have his right arm cut off. . . . His death was fittingly announced to his sisters by the giggling and spluttering village idiot.'

Koestler was now writing the second volume of his autobiography and wanted to check some data in connection with Attila. He also asked me if I happened to have a photograph of him. Surprisingly, I did have a photograph. I had his collected poems and it contained the photo of a portrait painted of Attila by Vincent Korda in Paris. In those days of the Rákosi terror it was impossible to do the simple and logical thing: to write to Budapest and ask for a photograph of one of Hungary's greatest poets (although he was very much a *persona grata* by then and his Trotskyite deviation as well as his expulsion from the Party was conveniently forgotten). It was the photograph in my possession which was eventually reproduced in *The Invisible Writing*.

Koestler asked me if I had ever tried to translate any of Attila's poems into English. No, I had not. He confessed – somewhat sheepishly – that he had tried. I asked him to show me the translations which, after some hesitation, he did. I told him that he mixed up the metre but that otherwise the translations were rather good. He grew more and more enthusiastic: 'Why don't we, you and I, translate a number of Attila's poems?'

The idea appealed to me, and during the next few

weeks we worked busily on these translations. We never contemplated publishing our efforts but both of our publishers – Harold Harris of Hutchinsons and André Deutsch – showed interest. Arthur suggested that he should translate all the poems and I should write an introductory essay. I told him that this did not strike me as the best of plans. His essays were – to put it mildly – better than mine, while my translations were better than his. Although I had never written any serious poetry, I had written innumerable songs, sketches, light verses – even a comic opera – and I had a certain aptitude for versification and translation. In Hungary the translation of poetry developed into a great art. The English are rich in great poets, the whole world understands their language and they do not *need* to translate even Goethe or Leopardi – not to speak of Hungarian poets. In any case, who, in this country, knows German or Italian, let alone Hungarian? The result is that English literature is extremely poor in well translated foreign poetry while all small literatures, including Hungarian, are pretty rich.

Arthur would not hear of my counter-suggestion that *I* should translate and *he* should write the essay. Clearly his view of my translations was the exact opposite of my own – and in any case, he remarked, my essay on Ady in *The Times Literary Supplement* was all right, and I knew much more about Hungarian literature than he, so why should he write an essay on a subject he did not know thoroughly? In the end we agreed that we would both translate the poems and would both write an essay for the book: Arthur on Attila as a person and I about his poetry.

We set to work with zeal and devotion. Arthur normally never spoke about work in progress but this time it was different. I never saw him work on anything with greater enthusiasm. He would telephone four times a day: 'Listen to this!' he would say and read a few newly created lines.

It was during those days that I first encountered his inferiority complex in its full splendour. He said it himself, somewhere: that other people's inferiority complexes were huts, but his was a cathedral.

Arthur and I were working at his desk, on which the telephone stood. My wife, Lea, and Lena Wickman, a Swedish girl and literary agent, who had come to join us for dinner, were sitting on the sofa behind us. On previous occasions, having finished work, we went down to the kitchen, raided the fridge and had a good, cold snack. Arthur suggested that on this occasion we should go out, and we all agreed. We decided on a restaurant, whereupon Arthur turned to Lena, whose English is perfect, and bade her ring up and book a table. As we were still at work and the telephone was right in front of our noses, Lena was reluctant to disturb us and did not move. A few minutes later, Arthur turned to my wife – who has a hardly noticeable foreign accent – and asked her to do it. She did not move either, for the same reason. Ten minutes passed and Arthur turned to me: 'Gyuri,' (he always used the Hungarian version of my name) 'book a table.'

'I shall with pleasure,' I answered, 'but do tell me why you turn to Lena, to Lea, and then to me, instead of grabbing the phone and booking a table yourself?'

He looked at me almost sadly: 'What sort of table would we get if I rang up with my accent?'

I was astonished.

'They would put out a sign in front of the restaurant: ARTHUR KOESTLER IS DINING HERE.'

'You are a fool,' he said. 'We stay in for dinner.'

A few weeks later we had enough poems translated to make up a little book. Before sitting down to the essays, Arthur decided to consult his friend Auden on the subject. Auden had just been appointed Professor of Poetry at Oxford, so Arthur called Oxford. No one could help. People did not know where Auden was, nor even *who* he was. Whenever Arthur said the name of Auden to a telephonist or a college porter he had to spell it. He spelt it about twenty times, then gave up.

But he got hold of Auden a few days later, met him and showed him the translations.

'I asked him,' he informed me later, 'whether these translations convey the impression that their author was

12

one of the greatest poets of the century.'

He paused.

'And what did Auden say?' I had to prompt him.

'He is a polite man. All he said was: "No, they don't".'

That was the end of our first – and last – common literary enterprise.

SONS OF HUNGARY

Soon I became Arthur's Hungarian friend: not just a friend who happened to be Hungarian, but someone who had a special function, played a role and fulfilled a need.

In those days he still had several Hungarian friends. One of them was Egon P, a former general practitioner turned psychiatrist. Being bitten by the Freudian bug can be quite dangerous and in his case it was.

I had heard of Egon before I met him in Arthur's house. My wife, in the days before she became my wife, had been to see him with a sore throat. Egon started asking questions about her psyche and concluded that there was nothing wrong with her throat but that her love-life was unhappy. Upon which Lea left him never to return and went to a doctor who gave her throat pastilles.

Arthur told me a similar story about Egon, but on a much grander and more heroic scale.

In 1948 Arthur travelled to Israel to witness the War of Independence. Much later, he spoke to Egon of his experiences. He was travelling in Israel with some friends, in a jeep, when they were stopped by Haganah troops. Jeeps were scarce and badly needed. The Haganah, without much ado, ordered Koestler and his friends to get out, walk to a nearby wall and hold up their hands.

'It was not a pleasant experience at all,' Koestler told Egon. 'I knew they wanted the jeep and I was resigned to its confiscation. But I was absolutely certain that having stolen it, they would want to get rid of the witnesses, so they would shoot all four of us on the spot. I had been in some sticky situations but I must confess that I had never been so frightened in my life.'

'I shall explain to you why,' Egon said, to Arthur's mild surprise. He thought he knew why.

'You identified your virility with that jeep,' said Egon. 'The jeep was your sexual organ, your manliness. To be deprived of the jeep meant castration for you, that's why you were so terrified.'

'You don't think,' Arthur asked, 'that standing by the wall with my hands up, listening to the clattering of those Haganah guns, I was simply and plainly afraid of being shot dead?'

Egon pursed his lips and declared with the utmost contempt: 'Rationalisation!'

Another close Hungarian friend of Arthur's was Paul Ignotus. They had known each other in Budapest. Paul was a successful journalist, essayist, editor and literary guru, an eminent and much respected man and a brave fighter against Nazism, while Arthur in those days was a penniless half-refugee, completely unknown in Hungary, who was hoping to sell a play of his to one of the Budapest theatres (which he did but, in the end, the play was never performed). Paul was the only one among us 'London Hungarians' who had known Arthur in his struggling days and could regard him from the height of his own former eminence. When they met in London, Paul was working for the BBC. After the war he became Press Attaché of the Hungarian Legation. In 1949, although begged by all his friends not to go, he went back to Budapest to his father's funeral. He was arrested and spent seven years in jail. He escaped after the Hungarian Revolution in 1957. By the time he got back here Arthur was the world-famous writer and Paul had become the penniless refugee. This, however, did not change the texture of their original relationship: Paul was still the only one who failed to regard Arthur with awe, and he always had a bemused twinkle in his eye, as if saying: 'Look at little Koestler, didn't he climb high?'

Arthur's way of speaking Hungarian improved, he polished his language up quickly enough. He spoke Hungarian well, fluently and without any foreign accent.

15

But he was often lost for the exact word. He would ask me or Paul for the right word and it was no good offering him a vague synonym. It had to be the *mot juste*, however long it took to find it. Cynthia, who soon appeared on the scene, first as Arthur's secretary, later also as his lover, wife, nurse, housekeeper, cook, mother, daughter and inseparable companion, would always say: 'I'll leave you to jabber in Hungarian.'

'Wait a minute, Cynthia,' I used to say. 'We are only *jabbering* because you don't know the language. Unkown languages are always *jabbered*. Only when you have learnt them are they *spoken*. We are, in fact, *talking* Hungarian, not *jabbering*.'

Cynthia smiled in her sweet and gentle way and agreed. But whenever she withdrew in the next thirty years, it was in order to let us *jabber* in Hungarian. We never rose to the dignity of speaking it.

In the mid-fifties, the Hungarian football team came over for that famous encounter labelled later as the 'match of the century'. Arthur was a great football fan and loved watching the game. Whenever, in the coming years, I was in his house and sat down with Cynthia to watch Wimbledon, he always grumbled. An intelligent adult person watching tennis: what a ridiculous waste of time! But for an intelligent adult person to watch football – that, of course, was a very different matter.

On this occasion, before the big match, he toyed with the idea of joining the cartoonist Vicky and me and coming out with us to Wembley (we two were sent out by the *News Chronicle*), but in the end he decided to watch the game on television.

'Which side are you going to support?' he asked me a few days before the match.

I was taken aback.

'I am a British subject now,' I replied. 'My loyalties belong to Britain. Naturally, I shall support England.'

He shook his head.

'Patriotism is one thing; football-patriotism quite another.'

How right he was. Vicky – just as staunch a Briton as

16

myself – fully agreed with me and disagreed with Koestler. But that was *before* the match. After the first Hungarian goal – which came about thirty seconds after the
beginning of the match – Vicky and I stood up and
applauded. We were nearly thrown out of the press box.
In the press box you do not applaud at all. And most
certainly not the enemy.

The next occasion when Arthur and I found ourselves
to be Hungarian patriots – and not football-patriots – was
much more serious. It was in 1956, the night the Revolution broke out in Hungary.

At 2.30 a.m. on October 24, 1956, my telephone rang.
It was Arthur. He told me that he was with a friend, a
Hungarian journalist, near Eaton Place (the location of
the Hungarian Legation). They had collected a few bricks
from a building site and they wanted me to join them
immediately so that we should throw the bricks through
the windows of the Hungarian Legation together.

'I'll come, of course, if you want me to,' I replied, 'but
will you tell me what this is in aid of?'

'It's clear enough, I think,' he told me curtly. 'We want
to draw attention to events in Hungary.'

I told him that if he wanted to *do* something, as he
always did, if he wanted to *act* in order to let off steam,
and wanted me to be there, I would come. But considering the fact that all the newspapers were carrying huge
headlines about Hungary, and that radio and television
were dealing with hardly anything else, I believed that
'drawing attention' to the Hungarian Revolution was
somewhat superfluous. So what did I suggest, he asked
me angrily. Just to sit down and do nothing? Just to go to
sleep in our comfortable beds while people were fighting
and dying on the streets of Budapest? We would not be
helping those people – I insisted – by making our beds
less comfortable. Nor by throwing bricks. I suggested that
we should go to bed – or return to bed, in my case – and
meet tomorrow to discuss whether we could do something more effective.

There was a short pause, then he burst out: 'Damn
your moderation!' – and slammed the receiver down.

Next morning we read in the papers that thirteen bricks had been thrown through the windows of the Hungarian Legation. My journey would not have been really necessary.

The cry: 'Damn your moderation!' reverberated in my ears for years to come. Moderation was a major irritant to Arthur. Harold Harris, his friend, publisher and literary executor, told me that after Arthur's death he found some notebooks in which Arthur had put down ideas: aphorisms, apophthegms, and passing thoughts. As time passed and his illness progressed, entries became less and less frequent. In 1983 there was only one single entry. It said: 'Thou shalt not carry moderation into excess.'

That was the last thing of a literary nature he ever put down on paper.

The morning after our abortive conversation, I went to see him and we decided to call a public meeting in Denison Hall, near Victoria. The organisation of this involved long days of frantic effort, although we were helped by a professional organiser who did her job extremely well. The Hungarian journalist who had been with Arthur when he phoned me on that night, became a member of the organising committee. He was a born obstructionist and a bore. As he rambled on at endless and pointless length, I needed to discipline myself with the utmost firmness not to explode. I had always thought up to then that I had incomparably more patience and self-control than Arthur, but he – while he shared my views on the man – listened to him with courtesy and patience. When I asked him how he could bear it, he replied with a grin: 'My Communist training comes in handy sometimes.'

Arthur was determined to have a number of eminent people on the platform, not just the usual professional protesters. We asked (and got) Sir Jacob Epstein, J.B. Priestley, Henry Green, Hugh Seton-Watson, and, naturally, the name of Bertrand Russell came up too.

'Do you know Russell?' Arthur asked me.

'I met him once,' I replied, 'but I doubt that he remembers me.'

'That's good enough,' he said. 'Here is his telephone number. Ring him up and ask him to come along.'

I hesitated.

'Do *you* know him?'

'Very well. He was my neighbour when I lived in Wales for years and we often visited each other.'

'Then it seems to me,' I suggested, not entirely unreasonably, 'that you should ring him.'

He hesitated for a moment and then declared: 'Very well. I will.'

He phoned Russell straight away. The conversation was exceedingly brief.

'He refused,' Arthur informed me. And a few seconds later, after a thoughtful pause, he added: 'I was one of the co-respondents cited in his divorce case.'

'Good God!' I laughed. 'Why didn't you tell me *that*?'

He was not amused.

'A man of his stature should put personal considerations aside in such a case.'

Our meeting was on a Sunday. On the Saturday evening Arthur had the idea that we ought to inform the police. The Communists were quite likely to cause trouble, so we should ring the police station and ask for a constable to be sent along. So I phoned up the local police. I thought I detected a slight shade of amusement in the tone of the officer who spoke to me, but he told me politely that my request would be noted. When we arrived on Sunday morning we could hardly make our way into the hall: vast crowds thronged the streets and there were hundreds of policemen – some of them mounted – trying to maintain order. Hundreds of people were stranded outside the hall. Radio and television were there and the atmosphere was electric. Hugh Seton-Watson spoke on the background of the Hungarian events, then Henry Green said a few words and I gave the latest news from Budapest and summed up the situation. But the crowd was really interested in Koestler and demanded to hear him. The shouts of 'Koestler! Koestler!' became deafening. At last Arthur stood up and told the audience that he had just published his farewell to politics

19

(in the introduction to the *Trail of the Dinosaur*, 'Cassandra has grown hoarse') and vowed never to write or speak on the subject again. To everybody's regret he refused to break his promise.

* * *

That was Arthur's last public appearance as a Hungarian.

I returned to Hungary in 1964 and my journey kindled Arthur's interest. He decided that he, too, would like to go. While in Hungary, I was invited to the Foreign Ministry for a chat and I mentioned his desire, adding that they ought to invite him.

'Koestler?' one of the officials asked me. 'Surely you don't mean *Arthur* Koestler?'

'I am afraid I had him in mind,' I said.

'We have nothing against him', said one of the officials, quite a high-ranking man, 'but the Russians are . . . well, not very fond of him. We shall ask them. He is welcome, as far as we are concerned, but we are not going to muck up our relationship with the Russians because of him.'

I was impressed by this frankness and realised that Hungary was becoming a reasonably independent country. In the old days, when they would not dare to set up a factory to manufacuture toilet paper without Russian permission, they would firmly deny the existence of any supervision. Now they were confident enough to give me an answer which was, after all, quite reasonable and relaxed.

Some six months later I got an unexpected invitation from the Hungarian Ambassador in London. In those days this was quite surprising, and I could not guess what he wanted from me. We chatted about many irrelevant subjects before he broached the real one: he said that I had mentioned a possible visit of Arthur to Budapest.

'As we do not have the honour of knowing Mr Koestler,' he said emphatically, 'and as it was you who brought up the subject, I should like to inform you that he may collect his visa at any time.'

I told the Ambassador that Koestler was spending half

of his time in Austria and that's where he was at the moment. He replied that he could collect his visa at any Hungarian consulate.

I passed on the message to Arthur who was in his house in Alpbach, in the Tyrol. George Steiner was there at the time, taking part in some symposium, and Arthur, who got quite excited at the thought of visiting Hungary again, mentioned the possibility to him. Steiner was not too enthusiastic. He warned Arthur that few names were quite as high on the Russians' hit list as his. He must be number three or so, in Steiner's view. Arthur replied that on three occasions he had been short listed for the Nobel Prize, but he was prouder of his high position on *that* list.

He was never a man to be intimidated by danger, so he presented himself at the Hungarian consulate in Vienna to collect his visa. The consul received him with the utmost courtesy and was about to stamp the visa into his passport when he paused to mention one little condition: it was that Mr Koestler should not write anything about his visit to Hungary.

Arthur took his passport back and declined the visa with thanks. There was nothing sinister in the Hungarian's request. They just did not want to publicise to the Russians and the world at large that Arthur Koestler, the author of *Darkness at Noon*, was welcome in a country so closely linked with the Soviet Union. But Arthur – who, in fact, did not intend to write anything about his visit – refused to accept conditions. So he never returned to Hungary, after his visit in 1935.

His books were published in – I believe – thirty-three languages, but not in Hungarian. He always regretted this. When I returned to Hungary in 1979 (having been expelled as a spy in 1970) I talked to the director of a publishing house. They showed some interest in publishing an anthology of my writings. I suggested that they ought to publish Arthur Koestler's *Sleepwalkers* too – a completely non-political work, studying man's changing views of the universe and containing fascinating biographies of Copernicus, Kepler and Newton. I handed over a copy of that book to the director. My second

21

intervention in Hungary in Arthur's interest was not more fruitful than the first. A few months later I got his book back (and all my books too) with a letter telling me that 'economic conditions' did not warrant the publication of his books. Or mine.

In fact, Arthur's *Darkness at Noon* was published in Hungarian – at last – about a year before his death, by an émigré publisher in Munich. It came much too late to give him any real pleasure.

WOMEN

It has been said millions of times by psychologists, as well as by laymen, that one's mother is the most important woman in one's life. Arthur disliked his mother intensely (which does not necessarily mean that she was not, all the same, the most important woman in his life . . . but I doubt it). He was a dutiful son as far as financial support was concerned, which was easy for a man so generous by nature. As he felt guilty about pretty well everything, he naturally felt guilty about his mother, too. He often decided that he ought to visit her more often then he did, but found himself unable to carry out his noble vow.

His mother, in her turn, found Arthur a terrible disappointment. First of all, his first language was Hungarian – one can hardly call it his 'mother tongue', since Mrs Koestler did not bother, indeed refused, ever to learn it in spite of her long sojourn in Hungary. The relationship between Austrians and Hungarians used to be a complicated one during the days of the late lamented monarchy. It was based on mutual contempt – often a healthy foundation for a good relationship, which worked in this case, too, after a fashion. The Austrians despised the Hungarians as backward country bumpkins, but had a sneaking admiration for their wild ways, their temperament, their charm and their reckless courage. The Hungarians disliked the Austrians as their oppressors during former centuries, but acknowledged that they were a more advanced, more Western and more civilised nation than themselves. One aspect of these feelings was the reluctance of Austrians, especially Viennese

23

Austrians, who for one reason or another came to live in Hungary, to learn our barbaric (and very difficult) language. Not to learn Hungarian was the least they could do for their self-respect.

Later, in Vienna, Arthur upset his mother by becoming an ardent admirer of a new-fangled and dangerous creed. His Communism was to come much later, but becoming a disciple of Sigmund Freud – Mrs Koestler did not even condescend to get his name right and always called him 'your friend, Herr Freund' – was bad enough.

Much worse was to follow. Arthur went to prison, was thrown into a concentration camp and was sentenced to death. When they met, years after Arthur's famous adventures had been discussed all over the world, his mother never even mentioned them. She never asked what it had been like, how he had been able to bear the anguish, distress and misery, or even how his life was saved in the end. This painful subject was taboo. Young men of good family do not go to prison, let alone get themselves sentenced to death.

Mrs Koestler was a real lady and even a good mother according to her own lights. In 1935 Arthur visited her in a small village in Hungary where she was on a visit to some relations. Arthur, a distinguished foreign journalist by then, was invited to referee an important football match between the village team and their nearest – and deadliest – rivals. Arthur tried to officiate with great dignity. During half-time, when he went to chat with his mother who was sitting on a bench among the spectators, she started wiping his face with a wet cloth as if he were a small schoolboy and not an important and responsible dignitary; she tightened a scarf around his neck and admonished him not to run around so much because he might catch a cold.

Many years later, in London, an uncle of mine stayed in the same *pension* – a kind of superior boarding house – near Swiss Cottage as Mrs Koestler. Both the residents and the managers were well-to-do refugees, almost all Germans or Austrians. Mrs Koestler was one of the star guests. She was not too popular as a person but respected as the mother of a great writer – which irritated her greatly. All those people knew all the details of Arthur's dark and murky past and wanted to discuss them with her in a most shameless way: something which, of course, she could not tolerate.

When Arthur heard that I had an uncle in the *pension*, he asked me if I would do him a favour. 'I must go to visit my mother sooner or later,' he told me. 'Do come along and have lunch with us. I just cannot talk to my mother, it might be a shade more bearable with you there.'

I told him I would come with pleasure. Weeks passed but he never mentioned that lunch again. So I brought the subject up.

'I went alone last week,' he told me. 'I appreciate your readiness to come with me, it was a truly friendly gesture. But I decided that my mother is too awful to inflict on any friend of mine.'

I never met Mrs Koestler.

*   *   *

One's mother may, indeed, be the most important woman in one's life; yet, talking about 'women in one's life', we do not automatically think of mothers.

Arthur was often described as a womaniser. He had what in this country is regarded as an awful reputation. Iain Hamilton, his latest biographer, condemns him as a skirt-chaser. He implies (or at least that's how I understood him) that Koestler was a great man, an outstanding writer but that he cannot be acquitted of this somewhat despicable sin.

Most of his English readers, I feel sure, nodded and agreed with him. Some murmured 'disgusting', others, more forgiving, accepted the truth that even the greatest ones among us have their weaknesses.

Arthur most certainly was no saint. He had many faults, some grave ones. He could be incredibly selfish. Not in the ordinary way, as most people are selfish, but simply not realising that other people, too, had feelings, needs, egos. He was quarrelsome, he could be rude, he

25

was obstinate and occasionally obsessive. When I speak of rudeness I do not mean that he walked through doors in front of old ladies. Since he was larger than life in so many ways, his rudeness, too, could be stupendous. When he was writing *Arrival and Departure*, one harrowing chapter, describing the mass execution of Jews, was published by Cyril Connolly's *Horizon*. He received many letters in response, most of them accusing him of atrocity-mongering. He found one of these letters so exasperating that he answered it in *Horizon*. He wrote:

'In your letter you asked me the idiotic question whether the events described in the "mixed transport" were based on fact or "artistic fiction".

'Had I published a chapter on Proust and mentioned his homosexuality you would never have dared to ask a similar question because you consider it your duty "to know", though the evidence of this particular knowledge is less easily accessible than the massacre of three million humans. If you tell me that you don't read newspapers, White Books, documentary pamphlets obtainable at W.H. Smith's bookstalls – why on earth do you read *Horizon* and call yourself a member of the intelligentsia? I can't even say that I am sorry for my rudeness etc. etc.'

In later years he was not proud of this letter. He called it unfair and in *Bricks to Babel* excused himself by explaining: 'I had just received the news that several members of my family were among the victims . . . .' In this book, published in 1980, he does not even mention that the writer of that letter and the recipient of his counterblast was Sir Osbert Sitwell.

I have made this small diversion to show that I am not trying to cover up Arthur's abominable behaviour. I say this to be able to declare more convincingly that I find the charge of 'womanising' downright ridiculous. It is simply the result of different outlooks in different lands. It is not a different morality that divides the two views, simply different habits.

There is a world of difference between the Continental and the English approach to women. Arthur was born and bred in Central Europe and breathed in the morality

26

– or as most English people would put it, the immorality –
of his surroundings.

To start with, take the word 'womanising'. According
to the Oxford dictionary, it means to be licentious and to
frequent prostitutes. Prostitutes may be safely forgotten,
but the definition, even without them, is pejorative, you
can feel that the lexicographer was shaking his head in
disapproval. He seems to say (probably echoing Mrs
Koestler) that boys from good families do not have casual
affairs. They marry and remain faithful to their wives
ever after.

In Hungary we would never describe a man as a
'womaniser'. We do not even have a proper synonym for
the word. If we had, it would not have a pejorative
meaning. In Hungary, and everywhere in Central Europe, you would say that 'he is quite a Don Juan' or would
declare admiringly, perhaps enviously, that he has great
success with women.

In Central Europe every woman was regarded as fair
prey. She could always say 'no' and – after several re-
newed attempts to persuade her to change her mind –
her *no* would be taken for an answer, even if grudgingly.
But not even to *try*? This was a ridiculous notion, implying
shyness and timidity, quite unbecoming in a real male,
and probably offensive to any pretty lady.

In the last twenty years Britain has become a copulating
country but not an erotic country. The British do not
chase women. Perhaps they have no choice: perhaps
women say *yes* in a matter-of-fact and unromantic way
before the chase begins. Or else they make it clear that
there is nothing doing and the Brit accepts the decision
and turns his attention to other targets. Perhaps a growing number of men are chasing other men. (The 'gay'
movement followed the path of Christianity in this respect: to be an early Christian, and to be an early gay,
were punishable offences. Both early gays and early
Christians were viciously persecuted. Today being both
or either has become a matter of pride.) Perhaps – at the
other end of morality – a great deal of puritanism still
survives in this country. But Arthur (and I) were brought

27

up in a very different moral climate and it would never have occurred to him that having affairs was something reprehensible.

I knew of many of his affairs although he never spoke of them. Sometimes it was the ladies who boasted of their conquest, and often it was gossip, confirmed by observation.

Arthur almost certainly had an affair with Cynthia while still married to Mamaine. He had many affairs while married to Cynthia. These escapades stopped only when he became immobile and simply not well enough physically.

When I took Marietta down to Denston for the first time, I noticed the glint in Arthur's eyes. It was the glint of interest; the glint of approval; the glint of the old expert; the glint of the charming Continental rascal. It was no more than a glint, and it was a compliment. Cynthia noticed it too. Cynthia, although a strong personality in many ways, was a mild and gentle person, completely lacking in conscious malice. Unconscious malice is quite a different matter. When lunch was served by her she poured some green pea-soup into Marietta's lap. She apologised profusely and said she did not understand how it happened. We did.

STOMACH PATRIOTISM

I have quoted Koestler on football-patriotism. Stomach-patriotism is something else again but an equally strong – if not stronger – emotion.

Matyas Seiber – a dear friend and an excellent composer – told me once that there were three kinds of folk-music which were instantly recognisable. They are: Russian, Spanish and Hungarian. The same goes for Hungarian food. *De gustibus non est disputandum*. I am not arguing here about tastes. You may love Hungarian dishes or detest them, but you know, without the slightest doubt, what you are eating. Paprika makes Hungarian food as distinctive as the plaintive sound of the gipsy violin makes its music. Someone brought up on goulash will not easily take to shepherd's pie (and, admittedly, vice versa).

Arthur was a great stomach patriot and so am I. In the fifties we went sometimes to the Hungarian Csárda in Soho, a very good restaurant in its heyday, run by a man whom Arthur always called 'Uncle Weisz' although I believe Uncle Weisz was about ten years younger than Uncle Arthur. Arthur was extremely fond of a dish which I personally find not only disgusting but unsuitable for human consumption – a Magyar version of tripe or chitterlings. Everyone is entitled to his own preferences, as I have said, but smell is another matter. Arriving at the Csárda we usually asked for a very long table, so that while Arthur was consuming his tripe at one end, I could try to enjoy my meal at the other. I always found even the longest table much too short.

During later years I became a reasonably good cook. First it was necessity that forced me to try it, but later it became quite a hobby. My repertoire is a smallish one, but the few dishes I cook I do tolerably well and my cooking has as strong a Central European accent as my speech, which is exactly what both Arthur and I loved. And Marietta is a much better cook than I am, in the same idiom. So both I and Marietta were capable of pleasing Arthur at table, and this posed an unexpected problem.

Cynthia was an ambitious cook and she was determined to do her best for Arthur, who was demanding and sometimes caustically critical. But although a few of her dishes (for example her roast duck), were very good indeed, Cynthia was not a natural cook, she lacked the magic touch. Her successes were acknowledged with a nod, her mistakes were underlined three times with a blue pencil. Arthur sent her – in the early days – to a *Cordon Bleu* cookery course which improved her performance, but there still remained plenty of room for further improvement. She became pretty nervous about her cooking and the harder she tried to cook in the Central European way, the less she succeeded. Coming from South Africa, she could hardly be blamed for not cooking like the mother of five in a Transdanubian village. But she *was* blamed for it.

So what were we to do? If I gave Arthur a really good and genuine Hungarian dinner, he was enthusiastic and appreciative but his praise always implied a hidden – and occasionally not so well hidden – reproach to Cynthia: 'Why can't you do it so well, Angel?' If Marietta cooked an even better dinner or brought along a cake to Denston, this was even worse. I felt deep sympathy for Cynthia whom I loved; but I could not give second best to my friends. I could not deliberately spoil dishes just to avoid embarrassing Cynthia. She herself, always generous, used to praise my efforts and suffer in silence.

In 1982 we bought a pig. Or two, to be precise: two pigs. Early that year I went to visit my friends, the Schoepflins, in Norfolk, not far from Arthur's place in Suffolk. Kató, my hostess, who is a doctor, asked me to accompany her to the neighbouring farm where she meant to buy some eggs. At the farm I saw a number of geese and pigs and was told that the farmer was breeding them for sale. 'Why don't we buy a pig from him,' I asked, 'and arrange a proper Hungarian *disznótor*?' – a word which Arthur translated for Cynthia as 'a pig-eating orgy'. The Schoepflins were willing. The farmer was willing too, so we told him that we would revert to the subject soon.

These pig-killings – the *disznótor* – were features of our youth, ineradicable memories on which true stomach-patriotism is built. We kept dreaming of fresh sausages, black puddings, greaves – all absolute horrors for most English people. We were excited at the prospect of having a *disznótor* in Norfolk, but there was one snag: we needed a Hungarian butcher. Without a Hungarian butcher the idea was worthless.

I remembered vaguely having seen an advertisement in some Hungarian programme-sheet sent to me for some festive occasion. Not knowing that I might ever need the butcher's address again, I threw the programme away. Now I telephoned the lady who had been in charge of that publication to be told that she had left for Hungary – for two months – on that very morning. Then I called the cultural attaché of the Hungarian Embassy, to be told that he, too, was abroad. So I rang the Consul, apologised for troubling him on a purely cultural matter, and explaining that we badly needed the name and address of that Hungarian butcher. The Consul told me that he, too, was off to Hungary the next day, but he fully appreciated that this was indeed an important cultural problem and promised to trace the Hungarian butcher for me before his departure. He was as good as his word. Later that day he gave me the name and telephone number of Mr János Perity at Redhill, Surrey.

As I could not entrust our pig to someone personally unknown to me, I telephoned him for an appointment and drove down, with Marietta, to Redhill the next day. I found in Mr Perity not only a delightful and interesting man, but – much more important in this case – a true master of his art.

Emeric Pressburger, the film-writer and another dear friend of mine, asked us if he could join in the enterprise. So did Arthur a few days later. We became four units: the Schoepflins, the Koestlers, Emeric and us. That's why Mr Perity, in his wisdom, suggested that we buy two small pigs instead of one huge one because, he calculated, two pigs had four hind legs – four good hams.

We bought the pigs, left them in the care of the farmer and formed a Pig Committee. I was elected president with the official title: Captain of the Pigs. The first question to solve was: what names to give the pigs. This immediately split the Pig Committee into two. Arthur was strongly against the idea of giving them names. Names would turn them into individuals, porcine persons, almost friends, and it would be painful to kill them in cold blood. I strongly opposed these views and called them hypocritical. We must face our own deeds and either do what we mean to do with our eyes open, or else – if we found our actions immoral or objectionable – abandon them. As long as the pigs are alive – I maintained – we must treat them well, feed them generously and look after them. But if we were sentimental about them, then we should not buy pigs with the purpose of killing them. If we are the murderers of pigs, let's call ourselves murderers of pigs. A long and lively debate followed at the end of which I was defeated by one vote.

The pig killing took place on December 5, 1982. It was only a moderate success. We had some very good fresh sausages which Arthur – who did not come over but to whom we delivered his share – enjoyed greatly. But the Koestlers, a little later, committed a grave mistake. They received, about four weeks after the killing of the pigs, another huge batch of sausages which had to be hung up in a garage or some such place to dry. By that time they were back in London and they had no suitable place for hanging up scores of sausages in their Knightsbridge house. So they threw the whole lot away. I deplored their action and when I brought them some of our own sausages – as well as another kind, called *gyulai*, bought at a delicatessen shop – Arthur enjoyed them very much and he deeply regretted his impulsive prodigality.

Remembering our erstwhile and memorable visits to the Csárda, I often suggested that we should visit the Csárda's successor as *the* Hungarian restaurant in London, the Gay Hussar, also in Soho. Arthur was tempted. He kept his appetite to the last and remained an ardent Hungarian stomach-patriot. He always agreed in principle but, in the end, refused to come along. He was embarrassed by his Parkinson's disease, he did not want people to see his trembling hands – even though they did not tremble all that much – and his shuffling gait. He did not want to be gaped at and refused to appear in public.

So I stopped mentioning the Gay Hussar to him. In January 1983 he told me that a Swedish friend of his, a distinguished academic gentleman, was coming to London for three days; they would spend most of the time together and he had decided to take him one evening to the Gay Hussar. Would I ring Victor, the proprietor, and book a good table for the three of them. They got a secluded table and Victor, of course, did everything to please him, as I had no doubt that he would; neither had I any doubt that the excursion, for one reason or another, would end in disaster.

I was quite wrong. It was a great success. Arthur and Cynthia rang me separately to tell me how wonderful the food and the whole evening had been.

I was delighted. Now, I thought, we would be able to go to the Gay Hussar together. Arthur had been leading the life of a hermit, I thought, and it would do him a lot of good to go out and leave his house once in a blue moon.

I failed to realise that this was not the revival of a going-out habit. It was a farewell to his favourite Hungarian dishes; the last flicker of stomach-patriotism.

DRINK

Arthur was a heavy drinker. Some of his friends thought he was an alcoholic because he was dependent on drink, he needed it; but I think this belief was mistaken because he could and did control his drinking. At all times, at least since I met him, he was very disciplined with the timetable of his drinking. On weekdays he never touched alcohol before 7 p.m. He had a whisky or two (or three) before dinner, vino (as he always referred to wine) with his dinner and a few more whiskies, or brandy or calvados – as the fancy took him – after dinner. Yugoslav plum brandy, Hungarian apricot brandy and French *marc* were also among his favourites.

Drink was an escape for him from the horrors of reality – and he found reality *always* unbearable. His excessive drinking caused him a great deal of trouble, the most memorable occasion being Christmas 1949, in France. He was caught and arrested by French police near Paris (he and Mamaine lived near Fontainebleau in those days) for drunken driving. He was alone and knew that Mamaine was worried because of his not turning up – he was a conscientious caller in cases of delay or change of plans – and asked the *commissaire* to be permitted to use the phone. His request was bluntly refused whereupon he struck the police officer. A few hours later he was released on bail but the police laid serious charges against him and the threat of going to prison for the fourth time – and not for political reasons, on this occasion – hung over his head. The press got hold of the story and created a world-wide scandal. The headlines were huge but most of the comments were good natured. Iain Hamilton tells us that one of the headlines ran: *Le Yogi et le Commissaire (Suite)*. But the Communist press went wild with delight. They felt they had got hold of an effective stick to beat the author of *Le Zéro et l'Infini* and show him up as a drunkard and a lout. In the end Koestler got away with it without going into prison, but the escapade shook him. He decided to cut down his drinking by rationing himself to three brandies after dinner. He kept to that rule. For a while.

In the seventies he was caught, once again, for drunken driving, this time by the British police. He was aware of being drunk and had pulled out to a side-street and fallen asleep. As he still remained legally 'in charge', he was charged, convicted and his licence suspended. The scandal reverberated once again, all over the world, and Koestler – a very shy man who hated even good personal publicity – was again thoroughly shaken. This time, however, he chose a simpler and easier solution; he gave up driving and went on drinking.

I was pleased and touched when I heard, after Arthur's death, from Brian Inglis and some other friends, that Arthur had often spoken of me and used to remark: 'He's my only friend with whom I never quarrelled.' True, we never actually *quarrelled*, but there was a year's or eighteen months' break in our friendship and drink was its reason. Not that he drank too much; the trouble was that I did not drink enough.

In those days the Koestlers (to be precise, Cynthia was not yet his wife) often had small parties. Koestler never liked more than four, a maximum of six, people around. On such occasions Arthur was unpredictable. He either made it clear to his guests at 9.30 that he was tired and they had better leave, or else was deeply offended if anyone even mentioned departing before four in the morning. This time he was in the four-o'clock mood. He carried around the brandy bottle every five minutes and refilled everybody's glass. I let him fill mine at, say, half-hourly intervals, which meant having more to drink that I am accustomed to or like, but it was my quite frequent refusals that he noticed.

35

Whereupon I was dropped. Arthur stopped telephoning me, and Cynthia was instructed to be elusive when I called. Soon I gave up and our friendship – so it seemed – had come to an end. I regretted this but – as I do in most cases – shrugged my shoulders and accepted the facts. 'Such things do happen,' I thought, but I wondered why it had happened. For a long time I did not have a clue.

A few months after that party the explanation came from Paul Ignotus – a lovable and indeed brilliant man in many ways – but a terrible gossip. Arthur had told Paul in confidence that I was a horrible bore because I did not drink enough. The charge was just. I quite enjoy good wine or a glass of brandy in good company, but sometimes weeks pass without my touching even a drop of beer, and if I tasted no more alcohol for the rest of my life I would hardly notice it.

When I was six years old, a local landowner at Siklós, my birthplace, took me and a friend out to his vineyard and gave us more wine to taste than was good for us. He made us drunk and thought this was a capital joke. My father – I learnt this only much later – was very angry and told the man off in no uncertain terms. Maybe it was this childhood experience that put me off drink. I suspect another reason – perhaps connected with this early experience, perhaps not. Arthur, and many others, needed drink in order to escape from the realities of this world; I, on the other hand, absolutely hate the idea of not being in full command of my senses. Never in my life have I felt the need to be the 'master of the situation' but, at all times I like to be master of myself.

A man who did not drink enough seemed to Arthur an unsuitable friend. I was put on ice. He often treated friends like that – usually for more serious reasons – and it meant that they were dead as far as he was concerned.

I was dead, too, but got resurrected.

About a year later I was dining in my club, the Garrick, and Arthur came in. He was not a member of any club – he regarded himself as totally unclubbable – and came as the guest of Ivan Morris and his Japanese wife.

The story here becomes bizarre and farcical. In the

morning room of the Garrick we suddenly found ourselves facing each other. I meant to greet him, but before I could do so he turned and went away – not like an angry man who refuses to accept a greeting, but like a man who suddenly remembers something which had escaped his mind and now goes to see to this important matter.

After dinner I left the coffee room and outside it I ran into Koestler once again. This time he had no time to escape.

'Hallo Arthur,' said I.

'Hallo Gyuri,' he replied in a friendly tone.

I asked him how he was and said it was nice to meet him. He said he was well, made some similar plastic remarks and we parted.

A few days later he phoned Paul Ignotus and discussed the matter with him in great confidence, which meant that I learnt every detail of it without any delay.

Arthur told Paul that he would like to make it up with me. Paul – the sanest of men – said that nothing was easier: Arthur should phone me, invite me for dinner and I would be delighted to accept.

But Arthur was too embarrassed to do that. Besides, doing something so simple and easy did not appeal to him. He suggested the following ploy. Without breathing one word to anyone Paul should organise a party to which he should invite quite a number of people, including Arthur and me. (Arthur insisted on paying all the expenses.) As the most important thing was that we two should meet, Paul should clear the date of the party with me, before inviting anyone else. Arthur asked Paul to be very diplomatic. Paul rang me up and told me the whole story. We were amazed by this schoolboyish attitude but we had to keep straight faces.

Arthur arrived rather late at the party. About twenty minutes after his arrival, as he still ignored me, I went up to him and greeted him as one greets an old friend. He was obviously embarrassed. He told me that he was pleased to see me and did not know why we had not met for such a long time. He had been very busy, he said. Yes, it must have been that, I agreed. We left it at that, but half

37

an hour later he came to me to say good bye, telling me that he was just about to order a taxi. I offered him a lift. He seemed to be pleased, but with his usual modesty in such matters, he asked me why should I drive up to Knightsbridge when I lived in Fulham (we were at Battersea.) I drove him home and we chatted in a friendly way on neutral subjects. A few days later Cynthia rang me up and invited me for dinner. All was well again.

I rang up Paul, thanked him for his services, told him what had happened and added that while I treasured Arthur's friendship, nevertheless I would not drink more in the future than I wished.

I do not think I kept this vow. Looking back, I realise now that I *did* drink more than I wished, and more than I drank anywhere else. I never refused a gin and tonic before dinner, I had more wine than I meant to and I never refused brandy after dinner. I drank for Arthur's sake. And he, on his side, accepted with a sigh that I was a drink-bore, and decided to overlook my sin, even if he could not quite forgive it.

I might as well recount here the one and only occasion when, in turn, I was fed up with Arthur.

Before meeting him, I was in the United States where I had the honour of meeting Albert Einstein. Koestler's name came up in conversation and Einstein chuckled. Then, later, Koestler was mentioned again and Einstein chuckled again. I asked him what the reason was for this merriment. He refused to tell me but I got it out of him. Koestler had visited Princeton not long before me and over-reacted to the august company in which he found himself. Paul Oppenheim (not to be confused with Robert Oppenheimer, the atomic scientist) gave a party in Koestler's honour to which Einstein, as well as a close friend of his, a German professor of philosophy at Harvard and, indeed, Oppenheimer too were invited.

'I only smiled a bit,' said Einstein, 'because God Almighty knows everything but Arthur Koestler knows everything better. He explained to me what relativity was, he explained the elements of nuclear physics to Oppen-

38

heimer and the basic tenets of philosophy to my Harvard friend.'

Years later, Koestler invited me to visit him in his house in Alpbach. In that village half of the locals are called Moser, the other half Lederer. On my first evening we went to a village inn and met four or five Mosers. Arthur completely ignored me and Cynthia and went on lecturing the Mosers on agricultural subjects. He told them how to be peasants. All this in German, of course.

Next morning I was wakened by the church bell at 5.30 a.m. The ringing of the bells went on and on. At last it stopped at 5.50 and I fell asleep. I slept very well until 6 o'clock when the bells started up again. And they started again at 6.30, and at 7, and at 7.30. Then they stopped. I told Arthur that noise rarely bothered me and I could sleep almost anywhere but church bells chiming right into my ear at dawn were a bit too much.

Arthur told me that the Church had made a concession to tourism. In the old days the bells started at 4 a.m. but now they waited until as late as 5.30.

Next evening we went to the inn again. Another lot of Mosers came in and Arthur went on with his lectures. I had a vague feeling that the Mosers were as bored by this as I was.

'About those church bells,' Arthur told me on our way home, 'one gets used to them after a while.'

What was a 'while', I wondered? That night I could not sleep at all. I was expecting the church bells. They duly rang at 5.30.

I never got used to them.

I came for a month. I left after two days.

SCRABBLE

In the last three or four years of Arthur's life, we became passionate players of the word-game scrabble.

When we went down to Denston, we often played four games a day for two or three days running (playing before lunch, and before and after dinner). In London the routine was different. We went to the Koestlers (or they came to us) at 6 o'clock, we played two games before dinner, and after dinner – unless Arthur felt tired – we played a third.

Arthur was good at making up long and unusual words but the two ladies often beat us, all the same. The games were always friendly but not lighthearted – we all took them seriously.

On one occasion Arthur put down the word *vince*.

'What's that?' Cynthia asked.

'You mean "evince",' I suggested helpfully.

'I mean *vince*,' said Arthur firmly.

'What does it mean?' asked Cynthia.

'*Vince*. A simple word. You really should know it, Angel. A slight start when you are in pain. Or disgusted, or something like that. You vince under pain.'

'No,' Cynthia knew no mercy in such things. 'You *wince* under pain.'

Arthur was adamant: 'I personally always vince.'

After that incident we decided that you had to challenge doubtful words explicitly, declaring: 'I challenge that'. If the challenge was correct, the player caught lost his turn; if the challenge was a mistake, then the challenger lost his turn. So challenging became a risky business. You put down a word, say, *taxer*. We all knew, of course, what it should mean, but was it a proper word and – more important – was it in the dictionary? All the games, all the time, reflect the players' character. We, the three others, were careful and cautious in our challenges; Arthur was brave, in fact reckless, and quite often lost his turn.

On another occasion he put down the word *quo*.

I queried that. (This was still before the strict challenge rules came into force.)

'*Quo*,' said Arthur. 'You learnt Latin. *Quid pro quo*.'

'As soon as we start playing Latin scrabble, this will be all right,' I told him.

We looked the word up in the Oxford dictionary and the word *quo* was not in. So Arthur had to take it back.

In the next game I got the precious letter *q* and put down the word *quid*.

'Oho,' said Arthur, 'as soon as we start playing Latin. . . .'

Then he stopped and laughed.

For three years I hoped to be able to put down the word *holon*. This is a philosophical notion invented by Arthur, indeed, the very word was invented by him. It is not in the dictionary. He may or may not have accepted it. I could never find it out: I could never put the letters together.

CYNTHIA

I told Cynthia once that although I met Arthur in 1952, she – according to my best recollection – did not appear on the scene for quite a few years.

'But I was there, pretty much in the background,' she told me with a smile which was a little shy, even though almost thirty years had passed. This was about the most 'indiscreet' remark I ever heard from her concerning her relationship with Arthur. Not that she was secretive. Whenever I asked a straight question about her South African childhood or about her family, I got a straight answer. She was quite pleased to talk about these matters. She was intelligent, open-hearted, kind, very pretty and completely lacked malice. She did not talk about herself because she regarded the subject as unimportant and uninteresting. She was Arthur's appendix and – according to her – that was her role in life. She was content with that role.

A *Festschrift* appeared on Arthur's seventieth birthday in 1975 (*Astride the Two Cultures*) to which Cynthia contributed a chapter, 'Twenty-Five Writing Years'. The very title of the piece is characteristic. It was, of course, Arthur who did the writing but that was all that mattered. But she is, in that piece, rather close-mouthed even about the details of meeting Arthur.

What happened is this. As a young girl in South Africa she decided that she wanted to become the secretary of an author. From quite a young age this was her aim in life. She was in Paris during the late forties and saw an advertisement in the *New York Herald Tribune*'s European

Edition, in which an author was looking for a part-time secretary. She answered the advertisement and that's how she met Koestler, then living near Fontainebleau with Mamaine. Every week she travelled to Fontaine le Port, on the Seine, to type the last instalment of *The Age of Longing*. About this she writes: 'I could hardly wait for the next [chapter]. It reminded me of my childhood, when every Thursday my father used to bring home my favourite comics — *Tiger Tim*, *Bubble* and *Puck*. In no time I had read them and then had to wait another whole long week to see whether Pat the Pirate would have to walk the plank. I wondered what would happen to Fedya, the hero of *The Age of Longing*, and to the heroine, Hydie.'

This sentence is the single personal revelation about her childhood memories, indeed, about her life. The rest of the piece is all about Arthur. The first person singular is there, all right, but only to tell how she worked with Arthur on subsequent books. Harold Harris told me that he found among the Koestler's papers the beginning of an autobiography written by Cynthia. Having written a few chapters, Arthur and Cynthia must have discussed her work and decided to write a joint autobiographical work: one chapter to be written by her, the next by him. There are about six alternating chapters altogether, then they abandoned the project. Harold told me that Cynthia wrote about her childhood (I quote from memory): 'I was born in South Africa. At the age of twenty-one I left that country.' That much about her childhood.

Then, of a later period of her life: 'I married a man called Patterson. The marriage was not a success and we divorced after a few months.'

That much about one of the great, dramatic experiences of her life. This, however, was not all reticence. Episodes of her early life unconnected with Arthur failed to interest her. She does not even tell us that her adored father, Dr Jefferies, committed suicide when she was thirteen.

Cynthia was thrilled by the Koestler household in France and delighted to meet all those famous and interesting people who kept visiting them. She became

43

very much a part of the set-up, as much a friend of Mamaine's as Arthur's. She finished typing *The Age of Longing* in 1950. Then Arthur and Mamaine moved to America and bought an island in the Delaware River. Cynthia came to London.

In 1951 Arthur wrote to Cynthia asking her to come to America and become his secretary. She gave up her job and her flat and ten days after receiving the letter she was on her way to Pennsylvania. Then a bit of toing and froing followed. The Koestlers returned to London where Cynthia, once again, worked part-time for Arthur. Then she returned to the United States for two years and became the secretary of Ely Culbertson, the pope of bridge. In 1955 Cynthia came to London for a short visit, to see her family. She went to see Arthur whose marriage had broken up and who was by now installed in his house in Montpelier Square. Cynthia's visit became a prolonged one. It lasted until their joint suicide in 1983.

All this devotion – more than devotion: this vicarious life – was poorly rewarded during the first years. I thought – and I was not alone in thinking it – that Arthur treated Cynthia abominably.

Her hours of duty were twenty-four a day. She did not even demand any time off. Arthur requested absolute perfection in all fields. If a dish did not come off, Arthur's comments were polite in tone but scathing in content. Having been reproved and told off in front of guests, her face became red, she stuttered a bit but regained her composure in no time and smiled again. When her cooking failed to improve to Arthur's complete satisfaction, Arthur sent her to cookery classes, but taking part in that arduous course did not mean that she was relieved from other duties.

In 1979, when they were staying in Denston, Cynthia suffered an attack of acute appendicitis. She was rushed into hospital at Bury St Edmunds and operated on. One of the other patients, whom I happened to meet years later, told me, quite outraged, that only two days after the operation she saw Arthur sitting on Cynthia's bed and she was taking dictation from him. I feel that my informant's displeasure was misplaced. Cynthia did not insist on being a *person*; she was quite content being a function, a figment. She was content to be what she was: Arthur's wife and indispensable help and companion. She was content to be Arthur's appendix and she was deeply embarrassed by the dislocation of routine caused by the appendix of an appendix. She wanted to be helpful and I feel that Arthur, on this occasion – by dictating to her and proving how indispensable she was – was really tactful and reassuring.

Back to the fifties. Koestler bought a mews house for Cynthia near his own house and, for a while, Cynthia lived there, or rather slept there, as she spent her days with Arthur. He told her in my presence: 'I love you, Angel, I am devoted to you and I'll do anything for you with the exception of one thing. I shall never marry you. I am too neurotic and utterly unsuited for marriage. I can't even sleep under the same roof with another person.'

Arthur was a great prophet. On this occasion, however, he was proved wrong. After the publication of the *Sleepwalkers* and *The Act of Creation*, he was invited to become a Fellow of the Center for Advanced Study in the Behavioral Sciences at Stanford University, California. There he had to live on the campus and this created a problem. Those puritanic Americans could not possibly allow that two people should live in sin on the campus. On the other hand, Arthur would not dream of going without Cynthia or even of living apart from her on the same campus. He was trapped. He sighed deeply and married Cynthia. None of their friends was told about their plans. They put an advertisement in the *Observer* (which became a news item, with a picture). That is how most of their friends heard about their marriage. All letters of congratulation were ignored or answered with a breezy and humorous remark.

In the seventies a change came over their relationship. The first sign of it was very trivial but it made a great impression on me. It made me realise that something important was happening. Arthur mispronounced the word 'covert'. His English, as the whole world knows, was

45

impeccable in writing, but his pronunciation could be unorthodox. Cynthia started laughing at him loudly. We waited a few seconds but Cynthia could not stop. She repeated the mispronounced word several times as if she had heard the funniest of jokes. Arthur did not mind at first but when the merriment did not cease, he remarked, slightly irritated: 'Well, Angel, it is not all that funny.'

But Cynthia found it all *that* funny. Her laughter became almost hysterical – a most unusual phenomenon in the case of that shy and reticent girl. At last she apologised and wiped away her tears of laughter.

A few years before she would not have dared to laugh at Arthur so openly and loudly. She would rather have choked. Or run out of the room if she could not control herself.

This uninhibited laughter signalled, for me, a new phase in their relationship. Arthur, having lost, and later given up, his driving licence, became more and more dependent on Cynthia. This increased Cynthia's self-confidence. At first Arthur would take a taxi now and then, and go off on various errands of his own, but these occasions became rarer and rarer and then ceased altogether.

When Parkinson's disease was diagnosed in 1978, Arthur became Cynthia's prisoner. When leukemia set in – unknown to all of us – the position became even worse. Cynthia was an understanding, gentle and sweet jailer. But Arthur – given to depressions at the happiest times of his life – did feel a prisoner. He did not rebel: he accepted his fate and became resigned to it. There was no bitterness in Arthur: they grew closer and closer to each other. But Cynthia was inevitably gaining the upper hand. Circumstances had changed and Cynthia was growing more and more self-confident. She teased Arthur – gently and lovingly – yet in a way she would not have dared a few years before. If she made a complete mess of a dish and Arthur grumbled – less offensively than in early days – Cynthia apologised in vague terms but, quite obviously, was not much concerned. There was a shrug of the shoulder in her voice. She had come into her own. Arthur could hardly move without her. And, apart from rushing out to do some quick shopping at Knightsbridge, she was never away from him for a minute, in their last years. In a sense Arthur had been beaten and he knew it.

All this made their relationship sweeter. They loved each other more than ever before. Arthur could not help but be touched by Cynthia's total dedication and devotion of which, in the end, she gave such dramatic and shattering proof. But Cynthia, too, was happy to live and die with and for Arthur. She achieved her childhood dream: she became more than the secretary of a writer – and one of the greatest of the age. Arthur, in a suicide note written in June 1982 – eight months before their joint suicide – when he thought that Cynthia would survive him, concluded thus: 'What makes it nevertheless hard to take this final step is the reflection of the pain it is bound to inflict on my few surviving friends, and above all my wife Cynthia. It is to her that I owe the relative peace and happiness that I enjoyed in the last period of my life – and never before.'

Eight months later, when it came to the final act, roles changed once again most dramatically. In their last few years Arthur could not go out alone; neither out of the Knightsbridge house, nor out of the Denston garden. And finally he could not go out alone from their lives, which had truly become one single life.

DAVID AND KOPPERNIGK

One day I visited Arthur and found an academic gentleman there. Arthur in those days was engaged in writing *The Sleepwalkers* and the two were discussing Copernicus to whom Arthur kept referring, somewhat contemptuously, as Canon Koppernigk (which was his real name).

I was fascinated by listening to their conversation. It was not the main subject that intrigued me. *The Sleepwalkers* – as we all know now – contains three brilliant biographies. Kepler Arthur loved, he used to be one of his childhood heroes; Newton he admired; Copernicus he detested. It became clear from their discussion that Arthur thought the Canon timid, in fact, a coward. He also thought that his theory of epicycles was plain silly. He regarded him as lazy. He had made only about sixty or seventy observations of the skies during a long lifetime and regarded this as more than sufficient, which Arthur did not. Copernicus was a philosopher and mathematician, so he deemed mere observation beneath his dignity. Even the position he assumed for his basic star, the Spica, which he used as a landmark, was wrong by about forty minutes arc, 'more than the width of the moon'.

In the book Koestler summed up his views: '. . . if memory could lend some deceptive warmth and colour to Canon Koppernigk's past, its soothing grace does not extend to posterity. Copernicus is perhaps the most colourless figure among those who, by merit or circumstances, shaped mankind's destiny. On the luminous sky of the Renaissance he appears as one of those dark stars whose existence is only revealed by their powerful radiations.'

He wrote of many astronomers in that book and he could not love them all. What surprised, even astonished me, while listening to that discussion, was not his low opinion of the Canon or even his determination to debunk him, but his passionate fury. He was as emotional and angry with Copernicus as though they had just had a nasty, personal quarrel in one of the cafés of Budapest or Vienna.

This passionate involvement was, of course, as characteristic of Koestler as detached laziness was of Canon Koppernigk. No book and few articles have ever appeared about Koestler which failed to mention the good causes he fought for. The truth is that everything was a cause for him. He placed everything into a wider perspective, everything had a much deeper meaning to him than to us, more superficial beings. Everything was either depressing or inspiring – usually depressing. The problems may have been burning issues or just regrettable aberrations, vital causes or minor vexations, traumatic curses or annoying mishaps – they all mattered and seemed to have a bearing on human destiny.

It has often been said – rightly – that some of the great humanitarians have loved humanity at large but could spare little feeling for individuals – even for those very close to them.

Arthur was not one of those. When I had troubles with my eyes (and I shall have a little more to say about this in the next chapter) he was truly concerned and got very angry with me for neglecting this vitally important problem. Marietta is inclined to suffer from migraine and has to follow a diet. Cynthia was most considerate, learned the rules in no time and never gave her anything she was not supposed to have, but Arthur, wanted to go to the root of the matter and to cure her. He tried to persuade her to see an expert – whom Arthur knew – on biofeedback, and kept urging her to go and see him. She refused for reasons of her own but Arthur would not take no for an answer. The whole matter became a minor 'cause'; he felt it was his duty to persuade Marietta to do the right thing. Biofeedback was the solution, he was convinced. The matter became almost a tiny crusade, it was brought up at most meals. He *had* to do *objective* good, serve *her* real interests and even at our very last meeting he reproached her for ignoring the benefits of biofeedback.

Once he prescribed some remedies for me, too, although I did not even complain about anything. He had just discovered a miraculous pep-pill for himself – I think it was called dramamyl and it helped him a great deal. He urged me to try it. I would work much better and feel much better. I told him that I felt all right, thank you. Suspecting that I would not buy the pill (or perhaps it was available on prescription only), he gave me a handful, and I decided to try them. A few days later our own doctor came to the house to attend my daughter Judy and he saw the pills on my bedside table.

'Who takes these?' he asked frowning.

'I do,' I told him.

'Who prescribed these for you?'

'Arthur Koestler.'

He asked me if I could sleep. I told him that normally yes, I could sleep like a baby, but in the last few days – for the first time in my life – could hardly sleep at all. Did I think, asked the doctor, that it had something to do with the pills? No, it never occurred to me.

'I see. You slept well until now. You start taking these pills and you stop being able to sleep. But it never occurred to you that there might be some connection between the pills and your sleeplessness?'

'No. It didn't.'

The doctor told me never to take them again. The pills were meant for people who suffered from deep depression and he thought that I needed a depressant, not an anti-depressant.

*   *   *

I am not going to describe all the various, memorable public campaigns Arthur fought. I should like only to remind the reader of the most important ones (John Grigg wrote an excellent piece on this subject in the

Festschrift for Arthur's seventieth birthday. The title of Grigg's piece is: *'The Do-Gooder from Seville Gaol'*.)

His Zionism, Communism and anti-Communism were also campaigns in a sense. He was not satisfied just to join a movement or a party and serve a cause as a private or even as an officer: he had to get into the thick of it, influence matters and steer them in the right direction.

Turning to real campaigns, in the more accepted sense of the word, his most successful fight was for the abolition of capital punishment. He himself spent a hundred days under the sentence of death (not under a judicial sentence but expecting execution every day), so he was even more personally involved than usual. A number of other people – Victor Gollancz, Gerald Gardiner, Sidney Silverman, etc – had been engaged for a long time in this campaign, but it was Koestler who brought it to the boil, turned it into a burning public issue and did more than anyone else for its successful conclusion.

During the campaign the *Observer* published a pamphlet *'Patterns of Murder'*, subtitled: *A Five Year Survey of Men and Women Executed in England, Scotland and Wales (1949–1953)*. It was by 'Vigil'. The eight-page pamphlet was a miracle of restraint and careful research. The restraint – which made its effect even more powerful – was unlike Arthur; but the thorough research was very much like him. The pamphlet showed, most convincingly, that most of the executed criminals were no villains but poor, misguided fools, carried away by despair, provocation and humiliation, usually inside the family and were more victims of a cruel system than wrongdoers. This seemed to be true, even forgetting the Tim Evanses who were hanged by mistake. I asked Koestler if he was the author of the pamphlet. He muttered something about a communal effort. I refused to believe him and said it read very much like his own work. Then he stood up, took a copy from his desk and inscribed it for me (in Hungarian): 'Kind regards from the Good Old Vigil'.

His book, *Reflection on Hanging*, is a masterpiece of debating literature. I read it more often than any other of his books. It was very much the work of a Continental writer. It shook the stupor and torpidity of many Englishmen. Before the appearance of that book, judges in this country were treated with exaggerated reverence, like superior beings. They were never criticised in harsh words, they were regarded as sacred cows. Koestler attacked them violently, he criticised their conservatism, pomposity, reactionary tendencies often amounting to bigotry. He was particularly harsh on Lord Goddard, the Lord Chief Justice.

(I knew Lord Goddard well from the Savage Club and found him a witty man and excellent company. But that is neither here nor there. He was a cruel man, a disaster on the bench and if public opinion tends to swing to the other extreme, in this time of leniency, that is partly a reaction to the Goddard era. Lord Goddard has done as much for the abolition of capital punishment as Koestler himself.)

After the appearance of Koestler's book, many people started writing about judges in a tone which was unimaginable before the publication of *Reflections on Hanging*. This is all to the good. If all respect for, and trust in, judges disappear, this would be the end of democracy; but the respect has to be deserved.

The fight for abolition was the bitterest and most determined fight of his life. He was quite obsessed about the struggle. He kept talking of it – indeed, in those days he hardly talked of anything else. The fight reverberated through Parliament and the press. He was (falsely) accused in both Houses of misrepresenting the facts. Lord Hailsham threatened to report Koestler to the Press Council. Instead of being intimidated, he made complaints against Lords Hailsham and Mancroft (the latter an Under-Secretary in the Home Office). Koestler was fully vindicated, Hailsham and Mancroft were severely reprimanded.

'The singular beastliness of killing a human being in cold blood,' writes John Grigg, 'was not the only lesson Arthur learned from his period of incarceration in Spain. He also became vividly aware of the demoralising effect of captivity.'

The result of this awareness was the Koestler Award, accepted by the Prison Commission and subsequently by the Home Office, and endowed originally by Arthur. It came into operation in 1962 and there were prizes for prisoners for literature, painting, sculpture, craftsmanship and musical composition. The scheme – which grew and was slightly changed as time went on – became a great success. It has produced no masterpieces as yet, but has alleviated the lot of a number of people on whom society, as a rule, wastes little time except for considering them as a menace and a problem . . . which, of course, they are. Once I made a complimentary remark on the scheme but Arthur interrupted me with that charming and modest grin of his: 'That's only a simple and cheap way to perpetuate one's name.'

Considering that he had perpetuated his name in a less simple and cheap way, I do not think that he was entirely serious.

He also gave large sums of money to a fund – organised by himself – for writers who had to leave totalitarian countries because of political persecution or a stifling censorship. He gave the entire, and very substantial, royalties he received from a Broadway production of a dramatised version of *Darkness at Noon*. He called together a large number of writers for a meeting and for the rest of his life was angry with, and contemptuous of, some eminent writers who had been effusively sentimental about the sad fate of their exiled colleagues but refused to give a penny to their cause. He never forgave them, some of our most eminent writers among them.

One of his unsuccessful, indeed abortive, campaigns was his fight for the rights of British dogs and cats.

He found it irksome that he – and many others – could not take his dogs to the continent; or rather that when British dogs were taken abroad by their owners they (to quote Grigg) 'must expiate the offence and purge themselves of foreign contamination during six months behind bars'.

He wrote a piece for the *Observer* in 1962, emphasising that he was not campaigning for 'canine aliens', but thought that dogs born and bred in this country should be allowed to return without going into quarantine provided they were vaccinated against rabies. He wrote: '. . . nobody who has seen his once lively dog slowly going to pot in its solitary lock-up and had to pay fifty-odd pounds for it will break into cheers at the august pronouncement of the spokesman for the Ministry of Agriculture: "After the experience of thirty years, it is proved that this country is far in advance of any other country in this respect." '

(If this had not been the view of the Ministry of Agriculture, many other ministries as well as other organisations, firms and people in Britain, concerning almost every matter under the sun, Britain would not be 'far behind of any other country' in so many respects. But this is another story.)

Arthur continued to carry the banner of the Freedom of the British Dog for a few weeks, but officialdom stood firm. Even the RSPCA was against him and, for once, his close friend and ally, David Astor, editor of the *Observer* was not too encouraging and refused to mount a fully fledged national campaign, lasting perhaps for months if not years. So Arthur gave up.

In this abortive campaign, as in many others, he was inspired by personal experience. He loved dogs and had many of them in the course of his life. I only knew the last two of them: a huge Landseer Newfoundlander called Goliath (Golly to his friends) and a small Lhasa Apso by the name of David. The constant, haunting antithesis of his titles (*Arrival and Departure, The Yogi and the Commissar, Darkness at Noon, Promise and Fulfilment, The Lotus and the Robot*) spread to his dogs, David and Goliath. As nothing connected with Arthur was just ordinary and commonplace, the fate of these two dogs, too, developed into a traumatic story and a moving drama.

Arthur was a dog-man through and through – basically an antagonist of mine because I, to my own amazement, developed into a cat-man. I have never quite understood why one has to take sides in this issue and belong either to the cat-lobby or the dog-lobby but, apparently, these are the rules of the game. I think you can love (or hate) both cats and dogs and if I lived in the country I would certainly have both. But I do not live in the country so I have only two cats. One is a black cat, called Tsi-Tsa (see her biography, *Tsi-Tsa*, published by André Deutsch), the other is called Ginger, one of the heroes of the same book. Arthur never liked cats – in fact disliked them immensely – and my two cats were no exception. He tolerated them – just. They were not allowed to go too near him, let alone to creep on his lap.

There is one rule for cats in my house: everything is allowed. On the whole they do as they please. I have a large table and when I have breakfast alone, they both jump on it, sit down at the far end and watch me. They know that when guests are present and the table is covered with plates, cutlery and glasses and surrounded by people they must keep away. One evening, right in the middle of dinner, Ginger jumped on the table, walked across nimbly among the glasses, dishes and plates and before I could regain my breath, he realised that he had done something wrong and jumped off at the other end. Arthur did not say a word but he was deeply shocked.

He left very early after dinner, saying that he was tired. Perhaps he was; perhaps he was chased away by Ginger's abominable table manners. I thought he would never come to my house again. But he did. And the first thing he did on his next visit was to stroke Ginger. Cynthia nearly fainted with surprise. She swore that Arthur had never – never! – stroked a cat. This was a memorable experience for all concerned, with the single exception of Ginger. Cynthia went on referring to it for a long time.

Golly and David appeared in the Koestler household in 1972. Both were beautiful pedigree dogs and Golly won innumerable prizes until Cynthia got bored with the whole lengthy, tiresome and time-wasting procedure of having him groomed, taking him to the show and spending a whole day there just to collect yet another prize. The huge Golly was gentle, meek, obedient, and stoical. David was much more temperamental, impetuous and fiery. David kept bullying Golly, who submitted to this

55

treatment with good humour. Golly's sheer size could be a bit of a nuisance. When there were a few people in the drawing-room – Arthur always sitting in his chair, with its back to the balcony, Cynthia on the sofa on his left – Golly was exiled to the small balcony, pretty uncomfortable for his huge bulk. There he remained patiently for a long time. When he definitely had had enough, or something caught his attention and excited him, he started barking. His barking sounded like naval guns and shattered everybody's nerves in Montpelier Square and beyond, so Golly had to be readmitted into the family circle.

If Cynthia was a human angel (if that be the proper zoological or hagiographical definition) Golly was a canine one. This was everybody's impression until the drama at Denston. The canine angel, without any apparent reason, provocation or warning, attacked the human angel with such venom and ferocity that Cynthia needed twenty-seven stitches. Gentle, sweet obedient Golly was sentenced to death by the greatest champion of the abolishment of capital punishment and was executed by the local vet.

The Koestler household was, after that, for a long time, plunged into deep gloom. Cynthia told me that David suffered most. Not only had he lost his friend and bullying subject, but he totally failed to grasp what had happened. He got over the immediate shock in due course, but he never really recovered. He was never again the same spirited and mischievous little David, for the rest of his life.

When the Koestlers decided to end their own lives, David, too, was condemned to die. He would have suffered another bitter and crushing blow, his life would have been utter misery without them. Cynthia projected her own feelings onto the dog. She was convinced that David – had he been able to choose – would not want to survive in new surroundings, among strangers, without Arthur and herself. And without Golly.

On Tuesday, March 1, 1983, Cynthia took David to the vet and explained (she was calm and collected) that her husband was too ill and it was getting impossible to look

56

after the dog who was, anyway, getting too old himself (David was eleven). They decided – she explained – with great regret, that David had to be put to sleep. She paid the fee and left.

David died that day. So did Arthur and Cynthia.

WRITER AND SCIENTIST

Arthur's public persona consisted of three layers – or perhaps one should say more accurately: he was Janus, looking in three directions. There was the writer, the scientist and, in the last decade or so, the man absorbed in parapsychology.

The last great annoyance of his life was Iain Hamilton's biography of him. Hamilton is not only a very decent and likeable person but also a good writer, and Arthur chose him for a biographer, agreeing to co-operate with him and give him most of his private papers because he had found Iain's review of *The Ghost in the Machine* most intelligent and perceptive. The book was in preparation for a long time and when, at last, Arthur received the proofs he was disappointed and angry. Iain declared in the book – without equivocation – that he was not interested in parapsychology, so he would not deal with that aspect of Arthur's thinking – i.e. with one third of his main interests. Arthur also felt that Iain did not pay sufficient attention to his scientific work. This meant that in Arthur's opinion Iain had neglected two thirds of his subject. Nearly everything Arthur wrote in the last twenty-five years was on scientific themes.

An acrimonious correspondence followed, involving lawyers.

Iain sent me an advance copy of the book and as I was to drive down to Denston on the following day, I took it with me. This was a few weeks before publication. I asked Arthur if he had seen the book. He had not – not the finished product. After our Sunday lunch, he retired to his room with it, leaving me with the Sunday papers in the drawing-room. Less than ten minutes later he came back, picked up one of the papers and handed back the book to me, with the remark: 'Enough of that.'

Iain was upset too. I spoke to him after Arthur's death. He told me that he had had no idea that Arthur was suffering from Parkinson's disease. That ailment – he added – was treated with a medicine which made the takers of it irritable and that must have been the real reason for Arthur's exaggerated anger. The fact is, that Arthur in the last years of his life did not grow more irritable but, on the contrary, much mellower.

All this was a great pity. Iain's book was a labour of love and it was a bitter disappointment to him that many years of hard work and devoted research evoked such a stormy response from his subject. Perhaps if Iain was not interested in parapsychology and his interest in science was only limited he should have chosen another subject for a biography, even if Koestler chose him.

*   *   *

If Iain Hamilton's book was Arthur's last private annoyance, his last outrage caused by public events, was over the happenings in Poland. He watched those events – the emergence and subsequent crushing of Solidarity and the humiliation not only of the Movement but of Poland itself – with bitterness, despair and anguish, and with the same personal involvement he felt vis-à-vis Canon Koppernigk. But he kept his promise of 1956 and remained silent.

*   *   *

Maurice Cranston said at the Koestler memorial meeting at the Royal Academy that if one writer of this age will be read by distant posterity that writer will be Arthur Koestler. I think he had one rival and equal among his contemporaries: his friend, George Orwell. For similar greatness, courage, breadth of vision, influence and importance we have to go back a generation, to the era of Bertrand Russell and Bernard Shaw.

Arthur received many honours. He became a Fellow of the Royal Society of Literature and, as I have already mentioned, of the Center of Advanced Study in Behavioral Sciences, Stamford University, California. He was inundated with invitations by universities from all over the world. He received the Sonning Prize from the University of Copenhagen, an honorary Ll.D from King's University, Kingston, Ontario, and many other honours from other universities.

I needed some help for a colleague at King's University, Ontario, and asked Arthur to put in a good word for my friend. Always ready to help exiles – although far from indiscriminately – he said he would write a letter, then added with his shy and modest grin: 'That is the real value of those honorary doctorates. It will be more difficult for them to say no.'

It is interesting to mention the honours he failed to achieve. He said about his fellowship in the Royal Society of Literature, referring to the letters FRSL, that the L was really one letter too many. What he meant, of course, was that he would have preferred to become a Fellow of the Royal Society, which would have meant the final accolade, the final acknowledgement that he was taken seriously as a scientist by other scientists. Some influential people, however, stood in his way.

Neither did he receive the Nobel Prize for literature. He would have deserved it much more than some of the laureates.

I did not and do not understand that omission. It is certainly not my fault. I, like a number of other writers, used to receive a letter from the Swedish Academy every year, asking me to nominate someone for the Nobel Prize. This correspondence started after the year Sartre refused the prize. I recommended myself, promising that I would accept it and would cause no similar embarrassment. I was certain that after such a frivolous reply they would not write to me again, but they did. This time I replied seriously, recommending Arthur and giving reasons for my recommendation. A year later I received the usual letter again. This time I wrote back, saying that I had told them quite clearly what to do and if they did not intend to follow my advice, why did they keep bothering me? Even after that I was not dropped. The following year the regular letter arrived. I suspect that the Committee was not annoyed by my tone because none of its members ever read my – or my colleagues' – letters. I think those letters go into the waste-paper basket, unopened.

Arthur got into the last six – into the finals, so to say – on three occasions. He wanted the Nobel Prize, of course – who would not? It was not the money he wanted – money never interested him when he had enough to live in reasonable comfort – but he said he wanted it because it would have increased his weight and influence and that was important to him. He never said that he thought he deserved it. But, of course, it would have flattered his vanity, too; after all, you have to be pretty inhuman not to be pleased by winning the Nobel Prize.

About vanity. Arthur was not a vain man, indeed he was almost pathologically shy and modest, and while he believed in many causes he did not believe in himself. I heard him using the word 'vanity' – referring to himself – on one single occasion.

(I have described this in my autobiography, *How to be Seventy*, so I shall give an abbreviated version of it here.)

When Koestler was seventy, in 1975, I was President of the PEN Club's Writers in Exile group. Our branch invited Alexander Solzhenitsyn to London and he accepted our invitation.

Before Solzhenitsyn arrived, I planned to arrange an anniversary PEN Club dinner in Koestler's honour. I hoped that Solzhenitsyn would be prepared to propose the toast. I asked Koestler if he would be ready to come along. He hesitated but in the end he gave in: 'All right,' he said. 'In this case my vanity is stronger than my horror of such occasions.'

Solzhenitsyn arrived a few days later and I asked him if he would come to deliver the speech. I mentioned

Koestler's remark to him. He smiled and told me: 'I have a great regard for Arthur Koestler but in this case my horror of such occasions is stronger than my vanity.'

And finally, talking of honours received or not received: in 1972 Koestler received the CBE, in other words, he became a Commander of the British Empire. I do not think he was overwhelmed. I rather suspect that he accepted only because he thought it presumptuous for a bloody foreigner to refuse it, as Evelyn Waugh did when offered the same distinction. Waugh wrote back saying that he was grateful but he would rather wait until something better cropped up. Arthur, as far as I know, never put the letters CBE after his name. We never discussed, indeed never even mentioned, this matter.

I am astonished that he (and Waugh) was not offered a knighthood. But this country is proud of its anti-intellectualism. I keep meeting obscure businessmen, dull bureaucrats, failed politicians whose non-existent virtues have been rewarded by knighthoods and peerages. Harold Wilson's resignation honours list (with due respect to the few truly eminent men who slipped in somehow) put the final stigma on the whole system. Wilson's publisher was raised to the peerage but the most distinguished writers of the era were offered CBEs. People who – to no one's surprise – turned out to be shady characters and downright crooks received high honours. It seems that it is a greater distinction to be left out of such lists than to be included.

*　　*　　*

When I have mentioned Arthur's scientific work to other scientists, some have been appreciative, others condescending or dismissive, while others again have called him a skilful populariser and added remarks like: 'Although I see no reason why scholarship should be entertaining.' Perhaps there is no reason for it. Neither is there any rule which demands that scholarship must be dull and clumsily written.

I cannot make any judgment of Arthur's scientific

achievements. I find his writing fascinating, often exciting and just as often above my head. There is only one remark which, I feel, I can safely make.

Today's science is becoming more and more specialised. People know – oh, not their own subject – but small sections of their own subject. People do not *know* biochemistry or physics; they know tiny and highly specialised segments of these subjects. In a novel of mine I mentioned a historian of the Thirty Years War, an expert on the year 1638. He had no idea why the war broke out; he did not know how it ended; but there was no significant or insignificant event during the year 1638 which had escaped his notice and in which he was not thoroughly versed. This was an exaggeration; but a slight exaggeration only. Scientists today cannot even follow their own limited field really extensively, they are so inundated with publications.

It is possible – indeed certain – that various professors of biochemistry, physics, mathematics, astronomy, ecology, eugenics, etc. know much more of their respective sciences than Arthur did. But no professor of chemistry knew more of astronomy; no mathematician knew more of eugenics; no biologist knew more of physics than Arthur did. You may patronisingly dismiss him as a Jack of all trades and master of none. Most people accept the fact that science has become specialised and that's that. But it was exactly that 'that is that' against which Arthur rebelled. He disliked the blinkers so many scientists wear so proudly. He tried to abolish the rigid frontiers between sciences because he believed in bisociation and even trisociation – seeing connections which the narrow specialists cannot see.

He wrote a great deal about bisociation. It means (here I must oversimplify a complex idea – popularise the populariser) to discover connections and associations between matters, problems, theories hitherto not seen as in any way connected. None of Freud's early discoveries were revolutionary. All the facts and symptoms had been known before him. He simply discovered connections between phenomena which no one had seen before. He

63

visualised a closely knit system where others had seen only isolated facts. This would have been enough (although he added much more to his achievements) to make him one of the giants of human achievement, one of the few who not only increased our knowledge but influenced our development.

Koestler was the last of the Renaissance Men, five hundred years after the Renaissance. He was a curious phenomenon in our age: he came too late. Or perhaps he came too early. It is far from impossible that humanity will soon discover that less narrow specialisation is needed and more Galileos and even Koestlers are urgently required.

THE MYSTIC

At the beginning of the sixties, I told Arthur that I was writing a novel, my first one. He wanted to know what it was about. I told him that the title would be *Mortal Passion* and that the mortal passion of my hero was eating. He ate like some other people drink – he was an eatard instead of being a drunkard. In the end he would eat himself to death, with suicidal purposes, on board a French liner.

'A good subject,' Arthur nodded. 'Better, of course, for Kafka or Dostoevsky than for you, but it *is* a good subject.'

This short conversation was, obviously, characteristic of both of us. It is not only beauty that is in the beholder's eye; humour, tragedy, horror, danger – well, almost everything – is in the beholder's eye (except, in some extreme cases, when judgment cannot be in dispute. According to the old adage, all coins have two sides. That's a mistake. Most coins have three, four or more sides; and there are quite a few coins which have one side only). For Arthur my hero's predicament was dark tragedy – just as it would have been for Kafka and Dostoevsky. But I could not possibly write the novels of those eminent gentlemen. I, while feeling compassion and a great deal of affection for the poor bastard, could not help seeing the less heroic aspects of his predicament.

This difference of approach, this different way of looking at the world was a source of constant surprise for both of us. He knew I was a reasonably happy man. And a happy man was a strange curiosity, almost a mystery for him.

When Britain made its first application to join the

European Common Market (as it then was called), *Encounter* asked a number of writers whether they were for or against joining and why. I gave a lighthearted reply, declaring that I was deeply disappointed in Britain's decision to join. I had given years, indeed decades, of my life to becoming a proper Englishman and now the whole country, lock, stock and barrel was to become a bloody foreigner, as European as I had been. I never expected anyone to take this answer too seriously and nobody did. I was and still am a good European, quite convinced that Britain's place is in Europe and that the Labour Party's present plan of leaving Europe might be good for vote-catching but is disastrous in the long run. But there was one hitch. Mel Lasky, the Editor of *Encounter* counted the votes: how many writers were for, how many against Europe. I was counted among those who were against. This made Arthur very angry. I tried to explain that if I had had the faintest idea about votes being counted, I would have added a sentence making my position clear. Paul Ignotus came to my help, explaining that I was only joking.

'Tell your friend Mikes,' Arthur replied, 'that not everything is a joke.'

'Tell your friend Koestler that not everything is tragedy, gloom and disaster,' I replied when I got the message.

*　　*　　*

Psi (parapsychology and related subjects) was another field where we could not see eye to eye – indeed, where we failed to understand each other. After some discussions, years ago, he never even mentioned the subject to me. I was a hopeless case.

I should like to quote here Brian Inglis, Arthur's close friend, with whom he discussed these matters constantly in the last fifteen years of his life.

'Some obituaries,' he wrote, 'left the impression that [Koestler's] interest in parapsychology was an aberration: perhaps a sign that his formidable mental powers were

66

waning. Nothing could be further from the truth.'

Arthur had five memorable experiences in his life – enumerated and retold by Inglis – which puzzled him and pushed him towards wondering about the supernatural. In the *Bricks of Babel* Arthur said himself that he had had some psychic experiences which, though of little evidential value, were subjectively important for him.

I have had similar experiences, and so have most of us. The events could not be pure coincidences, said Arthur; they could and were, said I.

He hated the cheats, the swindlers, the fakes and called a lot of what was going on 'pornography'. He wrote that in mini-physics and macro-physics – when we get down to the particles of the atom or out in space – our commonplace physical notions about time, mass, energy and many other matters become irrelevant and nonsensical. He tried to establish a parallel: perhaps para-psychology belonged to a micro-macro-world where our everyday, prosaic rules did not work. So he tried to find some hard and irrefutable evidence; or, failing that, at least, some strong, supporting data. Levitation was a notion that always fascinated Arthur. If under strong emotions one would lose some weight, he reasoned, then perhaps some people might lose *all their weight* and levitate. To prove that – or at least to make it probable – he had to prove first of all that under strong emotions or in a meditating mood people really lost weight. Arthur bought a very sophisticated weighing machine and installed it in the basement of his house at Montpelier Square, and made innumerable experiments. Although the weighing machine registered (on a graph) even the slightest changes in weight, there was only one case – the case of a child – when the loss of weight seemed conclusive. A grown-up man – in fact a fat man – under ideal experimental conditions when he ought to have lost weight actually put on a considerable amount. After that Arthur called it a day and got rid of the weighing machine.

He was inclined to believe in mysticism and I am not. He collected stories of amazing coincidence, and believed that it could not all be explained by chance. After the appearance of an extract of *The Roots of Coincidence* in the *Sunday Times*, Arthur asked for such stories and promised to reward the best ones. One of these stories became well known – perhaps it had been well known even before it was published in the *Sunday Times*. Abraham Lincoln and John Kennedy, two presidents of the United States, were both assassinated. Lincoln was elected in 1860, Kennedy in 1960. Both were succeeded in the presidency by men called Johnson: Andrew Johnson was born in 1808, Lyndon Johnson in 1908. Lincoln's assassin, John Wilkes Booth, was born in 1839, Kennedy's assassin, Lee Harvey Oswald in 1939. Both murderers were themselves murdered before they could stand trial. Lincoln's secretary, called Kennedy, implored the President not to go to the theatre; Kennedy's secretary, called Lincoln, begged the President not to go to Dallas. Booth shot the President in a theatre and fled to a storehouse; Oswald shot the President from a storehouse and then fled to a theatre.

Very interesting. But a lot of data concerning these assassinations does *not* correspond in this way. You may answer that the differences are irrelevant, it is the similarities and parallels that are striking. Fair enough. But if you examine the correspondences, what do they mean? Nothing. Did Mrs Kennedy senior, John Kennedy's mother, have the remotest intimation that a child of hers must be born in 1917 in order that he be elected president in 1960, even at the risk of being assassinated? The very question is too fatuous. Or does the story perhaps contain a message for a future president, to be born in 2017 in order to be elected in 2060? Possibly, but I shall not be here to check. In any case if I had argued with Arthur on similar lines, he would have dismissed me as a man with a closed mind who puts down everything to sheer coincidence and refuses to bow to evidence.

But where is the evidence – beyond such peculiarities? Arthur was searching for it patiently, sometimes desperately and he admitted that he had never found anything really convincing, let alone conclusive.

It is true, however, that Koestler's views were not cool, clear and unbiased. He *wanted* to believe in the supernatural. George Steiner wrote about him in the *Sunday Times*, after his death: 'Even close friends and admirers found the resulting brew of psychosomatic inference, mystical biology and murky parlour-tricks hard to swallow. . . . His public stance did cut him off from all but an eccentric handful in the very community which he most prized: that of the working scientists, of the Fellows of the Royal Society, whose respect, it not agreement, he ached for.'

The reference to 'murky parlour-tricks' is a bit unfortunate; Arthur never sank to that level. But otherwise Steiner's judgment is correct and it is probable that Arthur's dabbling in mysticism was the decisive factor which prevented him from achieving his dream and becoming a Fellow of the Royal Society.

*　　*　　*

I often told him that all mysteries were herring-mysteries. The story comes originally from Emeric Pressburger, the writer of many memorable films. Emeric was, once upon a time, a poor, almost starving, student in Prague (in the twenties). He became, a few years later, a well-known and well-paid script-writer of UFA, the European Hollywood of those times. UFA sent Pressburger back to Prague on some errand. This time he drove there in his own sports car and stayed in one of the best hotels. He was determined to enjoy all the pleasures of life which he had had to go without some years before. The first thing he bought was some rollmops, a kind of herring, which he loved but could hardly ever afford in his student days.

He took the herring to his hotel room and as it was rather hot in Prague, he put it to the coolest spot in the room, near the window. He meant to have it for breakfast next day.

At eight a.m. a pretty and chirpy maid came in, bringing his breakfast on a tray. She rolled up the curtain, layed out the coffee and milk and butter in a most appetising way, smiled at him, wished him a pleasant day and left. Emeric jumped out of bed, rushed to the window to pick up his herring but it was not there. It had disappeared without a trace. He looked for it in every conceivable place but the herring was gone. The only explanation was that the maid had taken it. But it was quite unlike Emeric to believe such a thing – which was in any case, extremely unlikely. This was a real mystery. Emeric had a lot of things to do so he left the hotel soon and returned in the evening. To his amazement, the herring was in its place, exactly where he had put it on the previous day. He failed to understand it, but was pleased: all right, he would have it the next day. But he did not. The same scene was enacted again and the herring disappeared as it had done the day before. This time Emeric set about searching for it with determination and even anxiety: he was very disturbed. But the herring could not be found. Except in the evening, when it was back in its original place, waiting for him as if nothing had happened.

By now it was out of the question to eat the herring; all Emeric wanted was to solve the mystery. If it *could* be solved, that is; because it seemed more and more likely that, for the first time in his life, he had encountered the supernatural. Five days passed and it was on the sixth that the mystery was solved. He had placed the herring on a ledge which he failed to notice. When the maid rolled up the curtain in the morning, up went the herring to the ceiling; when she rolled the curtain down at night, the herring returned.

All mysteries are herring mysteries, I repeated to Arthur. Mysteries with simple, logical and unromantic solutions. Or call them thunder-mysteries. Primitive man thought thunder and lightning were signs of the gods' displeasure and wrath. Today we have a simple explanation for this which any child can understand. We know more today than primitive man did; but, in absolute terms, we are still pretty ignorant and just cannot explain many phenomena around us. But the explanation – whenever it comes – will be natural and not supernatural.

Koestler would never accept this prosaic view, yet he was too rational, too logical and too honest to accept flimsy stories or flimsy proofs as evidence. He tried a new kind of bisociation: to combine fairy tales with scientific proof, mystical balderdash with macro-physics. He searched for evidence, more and more desperately. His way was the way of the sensitive thinker, the way of the troubled genius; mine was the way of the superficial and simple-minded humorist.

I still stick to my anecdote; he never found his evidence.

OPTIMIST?

It was about three years ago that I remarked to Marietta that Koestler had suddenly aged. He had started shuffling along like a very old man. Marietta disagreed and said the reason for this was not ageing but some illness.

A few weeks later, at Denston, Cynthia, in Arthur's presence, told us that they had decided not to be secretive about Arthur's state of health and to inform their friends that he was suffering from Parkinson's disease. She did not say a word to me (or, as I later learnt, to any of their friends) about the leukemia, which had also been diagnosed.

I was worried about him. I looked up Parkinson's in books and consulted doctor friends. Books and doctors were unanimous in their views that while Parkinson was incurable, the patient's deterioration was very slow when he developed the disease in old age. Some people, of course, were luckier than others, but I was hopeful about Koestler.

Arthur, as I have said before, was most concerned about his friends, and health problems were always of particular interest to him. More now than ever before.

In 1977 I hit a tennis ball into my own eye with savage ferocity and was warned that I might go blind in both eyes. Arthur asked me who my GP was. I told him that I was registered with a Health Service partnership almost next door, but apart from going to them to get vaccinated before American journeys (as long as that was compulsory) I had not seen my doctors since I moved to Fulham in 1968. Did I never go for check-ups? – he asked. No, never. But why? Because I do not want to become a hypochondriac. Once you start going for check-ups, they discover all sorts of ailments and you start worrying about matters which do not even occur to you otherwise. Very well, Arthur argued, but they might discover some latent illness and prevent it from developing by treating it in good time. Perhaps, I replied, but I think I know when I am ill. But if I am making a mistake, and am too late in discovering an illness, I have a plan for that eventuality. What was it? I shall die like the rest of us.

He obviously thought I was too irresponsible for words, or just mad. He stopped enquiring about my health, but when I had my eye trouble he was concerned and asked me who my eye-specialist was. I told him that I was in excellent hands. What was my oculist doing? Nothing in particular. (Indeed, this was the case. My very eminent eye-surgeon told me when the acute danger was over that he had considered operating on my eyes but had decided instead on 'glorious inactivity'. Nature, he added, if it decided to cure, did this thing much better than any surgeon.) Arthur found my indifference to my possible blindness stupefying. He had had a successful cataract operation performed in France and strongly advised me to travel to Nice and show my eyes to his eye-surgeon who was an excellent man, the best in France, he said, and one of the best in the world. I was grateful for his concern but refused to go or even seriously to consider the matter. 'Did you have a second opinion at least?' he asked impatiently. 'No. I am quite satisfied with the first.'

All this was too much for him. He kept returning to his advice that I ought to go to France. When I still refused, he asked me to explain in detail my reasons for this obstinacy.

'I may go blind or I may not,' I replied. 'I am sure that my eminent oculist knows as much about eyes as anyone else. And about *my* eyes he knows more than anyone else. But if I have a few more sighted years, I want to spend the time writing, even playing tennis as long as I can, and enjoying life in general. I am not going to spoil my life by rushing from one country to another, from one specialist to another. These few years may be a gift; I take them gratefully. If I go blind in the end – I shall face the problem when it comes.'

When my eyes recovered to some extent and the immediate danger passed, I had to visit my specialist every six, and later every nine months. Then my excellent Mr H retired and I stopped seeing his successor. Arthur – incredulous but concerned as ever – enquired, from time to time, what the oculist had said. 'Nothing,' I told him. 'I do not see him any more.' 'Not at all?' 'Not at all.'

Arthur, by no means a hypochondriac, regarded me as a very strange phenomenon. Well, there are all sorts to make up this world, his eyes seemed to comment. He kept enquiring about my eyes, but *his* illness created a problem for me. He disliked constant enquiries and resented solicitude. Yet I could not ignore his intimation lest my tactful reticence should look like a lack of interest, which most certainly was not the case. So I had to use my judgment.

One day I found him in exceptionally good mood. The doctor had just seen him and had apparently given him an encouraging report. His Parkinson's (and the leukemia of which I knew nothing) seemed to have halted. He asked me how my eyes were.

'As well as I can expect,' I replied. 'All I hope is that they will last as long as I do. I shan't need them afterwards.'

For once he was satisfied with my answer.

'I quite agree. That's all I hope about my illness. And for once I am an optimist.'

THE LAST CAUSE

In the summer of 1982 Arthur asked me and Marietta, during one of our visits to Denston, to witness his and Cynthia's signatures on a codicil of a will. The codicil was not attached to the will after their deaths, so they must have made a new will since then. The obvious conclusion is that Cynthia had not yet decided to die with Arthur, and was the main beneficiary of the will I saw; after her decision, they made a new one. About the same time, in June 1982, Arthur wrote a suicide note (of which I have already quoted one sentence and which I shall quote in full) and in that note it is taken for granted that Cynthia will survive him.

Arthur was a superb organiser. He often remarked, with a rueful smile, that his ability as an organiser was a survival from his Communist days. He did not always organise his life all that well, but he organised his death – their deaths – to perfection.

He told me once or twice (and repeated something similar in his suicide note) that he was not afraid of being dead but was afraid of the process of dying. But he was afraid of something else even more: of botching a suicide attempt. To be brought back to life after a *serious* suicide attempt must indeed be terrible. To all the tragedy which made you commit suicide, humiliation is added; you feel cheated by people's so-called benevolence and are made to look downright silly. In his case there was an added consideration: his scientific pride. If he had mucked up such a serious scientific experiment, he could not survive. (The phrase, that he could not survive survival looks, at first sight, singularly inept. It is not.)

I was invited to have dinner with them on Sunday, February 27, 1983. On Tuesday, March 1, their Spanish help, Miss Amelia Marino, went to their house to do her usual work. She met Cynthia in the normal way but did not see Arthur. It was after Miss Marino's departure that Cynthia took the dog David to the vet and arranged that he should be killed.

On the evening of the same day Arthur and Cynthia killed themselves. On Wednesday Miss Marino did not come and that gave the poison more time to work effectively. When Miss Marino turned up on Thursday morning, March 3, she found a note. It was written by Cynthia and read: 'Please do not go upstairs. Ring the police and tell them to come to the house.'

Miss Marino, in fact, rang one of the Koestlers' friends, read her the note and it was this lady who phoned the police. Inspector David Thomas and another officer went to the house and entered the sitting-room. One of Arthur's considerations was that Exit's instructions should be followed to the letter because in that case death would not only be painless but 'the body when found should simply look dead and not disgusting'. There they were, sitting peacefully in their usual places: Arthur in the armchair, with his back to the balcony, with an empty brandy-glass in his hand, and Cynthia on the sofa, on his left. They had both been dead for about thirty-six hours.

There are three questions to be answered. The first: why did he kill himself at the time he did?

Both of his serious diseases, Parkinson's and leukemia, reached an acute stage – as he said as early as in June 1982 – nine months before his death, and he was afraid of losing control over his own fate and becoming incapable of committing suicide. But there was another, even more frightening and certainly more urgent reason for choosing the date he chose and this is not mentioned in either of his notes. His doctor had discovered a swelling in the groin which indicated a metastasis of the cancer. He had advised Arthur to go to hospital without delay. That he could not and would not face. He was determined to die in his own house. He regarded this as a privilege and an essential part of human dignity.

Secondly, was Arthur morally wrong in taking his destiny in his own hands instead of bowing to God's will – as I have heard said by people I like and respect. One of the men who made this remark is an outstanding intellect, in Arthur's own class, which is why I have pondered over this remark, instead of dismissing it without taking it too seriously. But after careful consideration I still dismiss it. What if a man does not believe in God, as Arthur did not? Arthur himself answered this question. One of the most sacred rights of any human being is the right to life. This, obviously, includes the right to death. Arthur called it the right to peaceful self-deliverance: 'The prospect of falling peacefully, blissfully asleep is not only soothing but can make it positively desirable to quit this pain-racked mortal frame. . . .'. This was his last joy in life. This and that glass of brandy.

His death was not only his last joy, it was also his last cause. Each cause he championed became a personal problem; each personal problem became a cause. His suicide was not only a personal solution of grave personal problems, it was also a demonstrative act in the struggle of the Voluntary Euthanasia Society. In his most famous fight in the sixties, he fought for his belief that no man had the right to kill another man in cold blood; this time he fought for his belief that every man has the right to kill himself in cold blood. I cannot agree with religious people: Arthur's suicide was a brave and dignified act; and – most fittingly – a weighty argument in an important debate.

The third question is the most painful, and it concerns Cynthia. I have heard it more than once expressed brutally: 'I can understand him killing himself. But it was very selfish to take his young wife with him.'

No one knows or will ever know what exactly happened between Arthur and Cynthia. No one knows how and when Cynthia decided to die with him. But everyone who knew them well can see the logic, almost the inevitability, of her decision.

She was not the type to become the rich widow. She was

not to be a Cerberus, guarding her great husband's memory and legal rights. She was an intelligent and lovable woman who had dedicated herself to a man. And a strong personality, because only a very strong person could come to her decision and execute it with such dignity and self-discipline. Even Arthur misjudged her sometimes. He remarked once or twice that Cynthia was emotionally retarded. She could not make friends for herself, only through Arthur. Their friends, in turn, often commented on the fact that during the last years Arthur had become totally dependent on Cynthia. Many failed to notice that during the same period Cynthia became even more dependent on Arthur. In those last years they were never parted for longer than a few minutes. Cynthia had no life of her own; she lived through Arthur.

Arthur left a suicide note written immediately before his death. Cynthia added a few words in her own writing. These notes were not read out at the Inquest on March 30, but the coroner quoted Cynthia's words: 'I cannot face life without Arthur.' This is the clearest possible statement that Arthur did not 'take her with him' but that she acted of her free will.

At the inquest a few more facts came to light. Arthur Koestler and his wife killed themselves with an overdose of barbiturates. Half a glass of whisky and two empty wine-glasses containing a residue of white powder were on the coffee table in front of them, also a jar of honey and an empty bottle of tuinal tablets. Dr John Critchmore, the Koestler's doctor, said in evidence that he had never prescribed tuinal for Koestler or Cynthia. The coroner declared that the note written by Koestler made it clear that the Koestlers had committed suicide and Mrs Koestler's lines indicated that hers was a late decision. How late, we don't know.

The note written by Arthur in June 1982 reads:

'To Whom It May Concern.
The purpose of this note is to make it unmistakeably clear that I intend to commit suicide by taking an overdose of drugs without the knowledge or aid of any other person.

78

The drugs have been legally obtained and hoarded over a considerable period.

Trying to commit suicide is a gamble the outcome of which will be known to the gambler only if the attempt fails, but not if it succeeds. Should this attempt fail and I survive it in a physically or mentally impaired state, in which I can no longer control what is done to me, or communicate my wishes, I hereby request that I be allowed to die in my own home and not be resuscitated or kept alive by artificial means. I further request that my wife, or physician, or any friend present, should invoke *habeas corpus* against any attempt to remove me forcibly from my house to hospital.

My reasons for deciding to put an end to my life are simple and compelling: Parkinson's Disease and the slow-killing variety of leukemia (CCL). I kept the latter a secret even from intimate friends to save them distress. After a more or less steady physical decline over the last years, the process has now reached an acute state with added complications which make it advisable to seek self-deliverance now, before I become incapable of making the necessary arrangements.

I wish my friends to know that I am leaving their company in a peaceful frame of mind, with some timid hopes for a de-personalised after-life beyond due confines of space, time and matter and beyond the limits of our comprehension. This 'oceanic feeling' has often sustained me at difficult moments, and does so now, while I am writing this.

What makes it nevertheless hard to take this final step is the reflection of the pain it is bound to inflict on my few surviving friends, above all my wife Cynthia. It is to her that I owe the relative peace and happiness that I enjoyed in the last period of my life — and never before.'

*   *   *

Arthur had divided feelings about life after death. He spoke of a 'timid hope' for a depersonalised after-life. He never expected to sit in Heaven enjoying blissful happiness, but he hoped, vaguely, that he might leave some trace of having lived, a sparkle on a river, a fragrance, or a light.

79

I know nothing about this sort of after-life. I believe in one sort of, limited, immortality: to live on in people's hearts, memories and gratitude. I am sure that Arthur Koestler, far from being just a modest, unpersonalised sparkle, will be a glowing light, shining through the twenty-first century and beyond.

ALSO BY GEORGE MIKES

ABOUT HIMSELF
How to be Seventy

ABOUT US
How to be an Alien
How to be Inimitable
How to be Affluent
How to be Decadent
How to be Poor
English Humour for Beginners

ABOUT OTHER PEOPLE
How to Scrape Skies
How to Unite Nations
Italy for Beginners
Switzerland for Beginners
Little Cabbages
Uber Alles
Eureka: Rummaging in Greece
Any Souvenirs?: Central Europe Revisited
East is East
Tango: a Solo across South America
Not by Sun Alone: a Jamaican Journey
Boomerang: Australia Rediscovered
The Prophet Motive: Israel Today and Tomorrow
The Land of the Rising Yen: Japan

ABOUT LIFE
Down with Everybody
Shakespeare and Myself
Wisdom for others

ABOUT HISTORY
The Hungarian Revolution
The AVO: a Study in Infamy

ABOUT A CAT
Tsi-Tsa: the Biography of a Cat

NOVELS
Mortal Passion
The Spy Who Died of Boredom
Charlie